RAVING FANS

RAVING FANS

*A Revolutionary Approach to
Customer Service*

Kenneth Blanchard
Co-author, *The One Minute Manager*®

Sheldon M. Bowles

Foreword by Harvey Mackay

William Morrow and Company, Inc.
New York

It is the policy of William Morrow and Company, Inc., and its imprints and affiliates, recognizing the importance of preserving what has been written, to print the books we publish on acid-free paper, and we exert our best efforts to that end.

Library of Congress Cataloging-in-Publication Data

Blanchard, Kenneth H.
    Raving fans: a revolutionary approach to customer service / by Kenneth Blanchard and Sheldon Bowles.
        p.   cm.
    ISBN 0-688-12316-3
    1. Customer service.   I. Bowles, Sheldon.   II. Title.
HF5415.5.B528   1993
658.8'12—dc20   92–30255
                                                            CIP

Printed in the United States of America

70 69 68 67 66 65 64

This book is dedicated to the seven customer-service "Charlies" who have shown us the way:

Senator Douglas D. Everett
Gary Heil
Harvey Mackay
Dev Ogle
Tom Peters
Richard Tate
David Watson

Foreword

Successful organizations have one common central focus: customers. It doesn't matter if it's a business, a professional practice, a hospital, or a government agency, success comes to those, and only those, who are obsessed with looking after customers.

This wisdom isn't a secret. Mission statements, annual reports, posters on the wall, seminars, and even television programs all proclaim the supremacy of customers. But in the words of Shakespeare, this wisdom is "more honoured in the breach than the observance." In fact, generally speaking, customer service, in a word, stinks.

And no wonder. Look at how we've been training our managers. When I was in college, we took courses in marketing and consumer behavior. The assumption was that the public was a mindless group of buyers and that with proper advertising and promotion, products could be produced en masse and sold to naive buyers. Unfortunately, as I tour the country speaking, I find too many young managers still think this way. Advertising, product positioning, and market-share pricing strategies are all important. But when all is said and done, goods aren't *sold;* products and services are *bought.*

Since most service is awful, America is ripe for a revolution. Although we may not be following the mission statements and wall posters, the recognition of the need for customer service is there. More and more, managers in individual organizations are zeroing in on customers, and their success stands as a beacon for others. Five to eight years ago, the quality wave was about to break over us. We discovered quality isn't enough. Today the customer-service wave is swelling larger than the quality wave, and when it fully hits, those not prepared will be washed into history.

What success I've enjoyed in business, with my books, my public speaking, and the many volunteer community organizations I've worked for, has been due to looking after customers—seeing them as individuals and trying to understand all their needs. I wish I'd been able to read *Raving Fans* years ago. This book is Ken Blanchard at his best. And that is very, very good indeed. He and co-author Sheldon Bowles have taken an important, complex subject, peeled back all but the critical core, and set out fundamental truths in a simple, understandable, and enjoyable form. **Decide, Discover,** and **Deliver** will become your guideposts, as they have become mine, to creating Raving Fans.

I can't think of two better people to write about this subject than Ken and Sheldon. I have known both of them for well over a decade through our involvement with the Young Presidents' Organization—an educational association of presidents under the age of forty who run companies with more than fifty employees and $5 million in sales. Sheldon and I were members of YPO, and Ken has been a top resource teacher for this group since 1977. Ken has been my writing mentor and the initial "prodder" for me to write *How to Swim with the Sharks Without Being Eaten Alive.* He has an incredible way of making complicated subjects simple and leaving people with gems they can apply immediately. Sheldon, along with a team he would insist be given credit here, built Domo, a full-service retail gasoline business, into a customer-service legend.

Raving Fans may be an easy, fun read, but the message is dead serious. I'll be buying a copy for every single one of my employees at Mackay Envelope Corporation. Those wanting to create Raving Fans and enjoy future success will do likewise.

Thanks, Ken and Sheldon. It's an honor to be asked to write this foreword. I've only one request. Please, please, please don't tell my competitors about *Raving Fans.*

—HARVEY MACKAY, FOUNDER
Mackay Envelope Corporation
Author of *How to Swim with the Sharks Without Being Eaten Alive*

RAVING FANS

Panic. Palpitations and Panic. He was aware of sweaty palms and cold feet as he wandered around his new office, the Area Manager's office.

He had expected to feel the responsibility of the new job resting heavily. What he hadn't counted on was the President's advice.

Thinking to prove himself worthy of the new position, he had promised the President to drive for quality in his department. Total quality.

"Great idea. Too narrow a focus," the President
had told him abruptly. "Quality is how well our
product works in relation to the customer's need.
That's just one aspect of customer service. Customer
service covers *all* the customer's needs and
expectations."

Then she'd added in a quiet but firm voice,
"Remember, this company was built on customer
service. If those others had understood *that* they'd still
be here. I trust you'll do better."

The Area Manager knew that "those others" were
the three Area Managers who had cycled through the
office before him. Each lasting about eight months.
The Area Manager also realized that "those others"
had all known more about customer service than he
did. He wondered what chance he had to hold the job.

"The only positive thing about this panic," he
thought, "is that it shows I'm in touch with reality."

The Area Manager eased himself down into his
chair. He closed his eyes and leaned back, wondering
how long it might be before he too was ejected and
joined "those others."

As he thought about his future and customer service, he heard a small, attention-getting cough. He decided it must be his imagination and kept his eyes closed.

A second, louder, more persistent cough caused him to look up. At first he saw nothing. Then he realized a man was sitting on the couch. A stranger wearing sport clothes, and beside him, a golf bag.

"Ah, there you are," said the stranger as if he had just discovered the Area Manager, who, shocked to find anyone in his office, managed to stammer, "Who are you? I mean, what are you doing here?"

"I'm your Fairy Godmother," the stranger replied seriously. Then he added brightly, "As for what I'm doing here, I'm here to show you the three magic secrets of creating Raving Fans, the ultimate in customer service.

"Also, I'd hoped we might get in a round or two of golf. The heavenly links are so crowded you have to book at least a month in advance," he added with an apologetic shrug, gesturing toward the golf clubs.

"I'm not in touch with reality," the Area Manager thought. "I've already gone off the deep end."

"No, you haven't," said the stranger, reading the Area Manager's mind. "Nothing is more real than your Fairy Godmother. You'll want to remember that."

"You can't be my Fairy Godmother," the Area Manager challenged, "you're a man." That obvious fact, he decided, was irrefutable evidence that he was dreaming.

"I know it's a bit unusual, but I came in on the quota."

"The quota?"

"Yes," confirmed the stranger. "You see, Fairy Godmothering is traditionally a female job and so, under the Celestial Equal Opportunities legislation, the job has been assigned a quota. When I applied I was snapped right up."

The Area Manager gave his head a sharp shake as if to drive the stranger away.

"Hi, still here," said the stranger gleefully, lifting his wrist and wiggling his fingers in greeting.

"Well, then, do you have a name, Fairy Godmother?" the Area Manager asked.

"A name? Yes, I keep forgetting about names. Here people usually call me Charlie. Let's make it Charlie, shall we?"

"Fine. Charlie it will be," said the Area Manager, wondering how he would get this nut case out of his office. "You're here about customer service, then?"

"You could say that," said Charlie. "Although, in another way, I *am* customer service. It's all a bit tricky," smiled Charlie, "depending on how you approach it."

"Of course," the Area Manager said in a tone of voice most people reserve to humor the very young or the very old. "So where do we begin?"

"Why, with the first magic secret of creating Raving Fans," said Charlie, noticeably perking up. Then much more anxiously, "I don't suppose you'd care to continue this discussion at your golf club?"

The Area Manager quickly seized the opportunity to move the stranger out of his office.

"Great idea. I'd love a game. Let's go."

The stranger, if he could read the Area Manager's thoughts, gave no further sign of it. The prospect of a golf game so delighted him he fairly wiggled like a puppy.

"A game," he bubbled. "I haven't played in weeks. Look, I don't want to cause any commotion. I'll just meet you at your car."

The Area Manager crossed to his office door and was relieved to find Charlie following.

As he passed through the doorway he turned around, but Charlie was no longer behind. He did, however, hear Charlie speaking. "Meet me at your car. Don't disappoint me now."

The Area Manager, determined to find out what was happening, took the elevator to his basement parking spot. There, sitting comfortably in what had been his locked convertible, now with the roof down, was Charlie.

"I hope you don't mind. I took the liberty of booking a tee-off time; then I placed my clubs in the trunk and put the top down. It's such a nice day," said Charlie with a beaming smile.

Half in a trance, the Area Manager drove out of the garage and into the traffic.

"Fore," yelled Charlie with considerable enthusiasm as the Area Manager shot up the ramp and onto the interstate.

"Don't you think it's time you told me just what's going on around here?" demanded the Area Manager.

"Rotten service," replied Charlie. "Around here, around there, around everywhere. Service stinks. Nobody gives a hoot. Rude is in. Smiling's a sin. Nowhere is it worse than at your company."

"I know that," said the Area Manager.

"And you don't have the slightest idea what to do about it either," announced Charlie.

"I know that too," the Area Manager replied morosely.

"Well, cheer up, dear chap. That's what I'm here for. Now why don't we wait until we get to the second tee before we continue. Car travel isn't something I get to do every day of the week. I love to ride on an interstate and I don't want to miss a moment of it. Drive on!"

The Area Manager was too stunned to protest. He found himself driving to his golf club as Charlie had suggested.

As they approached the first tee, a short par four, Charlie said, "I'll see what I can do for your game."

Charlie lifted the club in his hand slightly to point it down the fairway and then toward the Area Manager. He did it so smoothly and naturally, anyone watching would not have noticed anything out of the ordinary. The Area Manager, however, noticed both the gesture and the slight tingle he felt on the back of his neck.

Still tingling, he stepped up to the tee and hit a booming drive that rolled up the hill in front of the green and trickled onto the putting surface. When two foursomes waiting to tee off started to clap, the Area Manager looked almost embarrassed. He had never hit a drive like that on the first hole.

Charlie took three to reach the green. Both Charlie and the Area Manager two putted. While Charlie seemed happy with his one-over-par bogie, the Area Manager was ecstatic with his one-under-par birdie.

The Area Manager decided if Charlie could help him with customer service anything like he seemed to help with golf, that was great. He didn't care if Charlie wanted to be Mother Goose. He was willing to take help wherever he could get it.

"Not Mother Goose," he heard Charlie mutter behind him. "Fairy Godmother. I'm not crazy, you know."

On the second hole the greenskeeper was moving pipe across the fairway and play had been halted.

"Let's wait over there where we can talk," suggested Charlie, pointing to a bench off by itself under a tree.

"So you're going to tell me how to have satisfied customers," ventured the Area Manager.

"No way," said Charlie.

"No?"

"No sirree. A satisfied customer doesn't count these days. Now, back when I was starting out in the service department a satisfied customer meant something. Not today. Today you need Raving Fans. You have to create Raving Fans to be successful."

"I'm afraid I'm lost," said the Area Manager.

"Of course you are," agreed Charlie. "No reason not to be. You're totally clued out. If you weren't, I wouldn't be here. Nothing to worry about. We'll have you right as rain before we're finished.

"Now, here it is in a nutshell. Service is so awful customers expect to be abused. Cold food in restaurants, dirty public washrooms, late deliveries, rejected parts, lost orders, lazy staff—it's all normal.

"Bottom line: People expect bad goods and rude service. Give 'em junk and they're not surprised. Just what they expected. As long as the abuse isn't any worse than they expected, they'll be back for more. They're not upset. Do a survey. Check it out and they'll say they're satisfied. Satisfied customers. Ha! Satisfied sheep, that's what I call them.

"The service at your company should be so good," continued Charlie. "Your customers are a revolt waiting to happen. They're only satisfied because their expectations are so low and because no one else is doing any better. Your customer service slogan should be: **No Worse Than the Competition.**"

The fairway had cleared. Charlie stood up and began to reach for his driver.

"That's not a very flattering picture of my company," said the Area Manager as he took his own club.

"Not much of a company from where I sit," replied Charlie as they walked to the tee.

"What I want you to see is that just having satisfied customers isn't good enough anymore. You don't own those customers. They're just parked on your doorstep and will be glad to move along when they find something better. Believe me, in your case it won't have to be very good to be better."

After the Area Manager hit a poor shot Charlie stepped up to the tee. His drive this time was straight and long. In fact, it went farther than the Area Manager had ever seen a drive go on this hole.

"Wow, that was some shot," said the Area Manager with genuine awe.

"It didn't seem fair to do that on the first hole with all of your friends looking on," said Charlie with a smile as he watched his ball drop on the fairway. "So I switched shots with you. You don't play in the Immortal Masters for a century without learning a thing or two."

Turning to his host, Charlie continued his comments on the Area Manager's company. "If you really want to 'own' a customer, if you want a booming business, you have to go beyond satisfied customers and create Raving Fans."

"Sounds good to me. How do I do that?" asked the Area Manager.

"That's what the three magic secrets of creating Raving Fans are all about," said Charlie.

"Great. When do I learn them?"

"Whoa," said Charlie, "not so fast. We've got weeks for that and I've got time for more golf. You just think about what I've told you so far and we can discuss it some more after the eighteenth hole. Now let's play golf!"

The Area Manager spent the rest of the game thinking about what Charlie had said. He had to admit it made sense. Good sense.

Service everywhere was awful. So bad in fact he had to admit that he too was easily satisfied. His expectations were low and his standard of what was acceptable was low. What had Charlie called his company's customers? A revolt waiting to happen. He could identify with that.

Then the Area Manager considered the idea of a Raving Fan. Imagine a customer so pleased that he became a Raving Fan.

As they walked off the eighteenth green Charlie said, "Thanks for the game. I really enjoyed that. I know you're anxious to learn the three secrets. Let's shower and then we'll get started."

Driving away from the golf club Charlie directed the Area Manager out the West Highway and told him to park at Spink Mall. He noted that Charlie led him into Varley's Department Store, whose name he didn't recognize.

"It's not often you see a local department store in a major mall alongside the big nationals," he thought as he walked up to the door.

"You're right about that," said Charlie, commenting on the Area Manager's thought. "There's a reason though. Varley's sales per square foot are nearly double the big boys'. Come on in and find out why."

Entering the store the Area Manager noticed that it was very crowded. They were greeted by an older gentleman wearing a neatly pressed blue pinstripe suit and a warm smile. "Welcome to Varley's," he said. "If I may, I'll pin a white carnation on each of you. We have free coffee today in the Garden Court on the third floor and if we can be of service, please ask. Thank you for coming to Varley's," the man concluded.

"That's some greeting!" the Area Manager said. "Other stores could use that system."

"Of course they could," replied Charlie. "All good customer service is a result of nifty systems. Now let's go see the store." With that Charlie was off down the center aisle toward the book department. "Your wife's birthday is next week. Time you bought her a gift."

The Area Manager had been trying to decide what to buy for his wife and wondered to himself why, if Charlie knew it was her birthday, he couldn't tell him what she wanted.

"I know what she wants. I'm just checking to see if you know," said Charlie with a laugh. "Go for the new Tony Robbins book. That's what she really wants. The only problem is they're sold out until new ones arrive tomorrow. But let's go to the book department and try to buy her a copy."

Feeling the perfect fool because Charlie had said the store was temporarily out of stock, he walked up to the book-sales desk.

"Good afternoon, sir. How may I help you?" asked a saleslady. He noticed that, like all staff, she wore a red carnation and a large name tag: LINDA.

The Area Manager asked Linda for a copy of the book.

"What a great book," exclaimed Linda. "I'm reading it myself right now. Unfortunately, we're sold out until tomorrow. Will you be in the store long?"

"We're just looking around. I expect we'll be here fifteen to twenty minutes," said the Area Manager, looking puzzled.

"That's plenty of time," said Linda. "I know a store in the mall that had some copies in the window when I passed it earlier. I'll have a copy here for you in fifteen minutes. May I gift wrap it?"

As they left the counter the Area Manager said to Charlie, "I'll admit I'm impressed, but I bet that book will cost me an arm and a leg by the time they buy it at retail and sell it to me gift wrapped."

"You'll pay what they pay. To the penny," said Charlie. "No one undersells Varley's—and gift wrapping is free!"

Looking around, the Area Manager noticed a large play area with supervisors to look after children while parents shopped.

Just then Charlie announced, "There's the escalator. The washrooms are on the second floor. That's our second stop."

He obediently followed Charlie and soon found that inspection was the point of the visit. "Washrooms will always tell you if a company cares about customers," Charlie proclaimed.

Entering the men's washroom, the Area Manager came to a sudden halt, astonished by what he saw. The washroom was nicer than the locker room at his private club. Soft lighting, rich wood paneling, and real marble counters left no doubt that at Varley's Department Store making customers feel comfortable was important. Beside each basin was a stack of white cloth hand towels and on a shelf under the mirrors were bottles of every grooming aid imaginable. A man wearing a white coat was polishing the mirrors. The washroom was spotless.

"Looks good to me," said Charlie, turning and heading back to the escalator. "Time to go. Don't want to be late."

"How can they afford to hand out carnations, go to other stores for books, look after kids, and have washrooms like that?" asked the Area Manager.

"You'd better ask Leo."

"Leo?"

"Leo Varley. The man who is responsible for all this. He's expecting us," said Charlie as he rounded an aisle and headed for the center of the store.

Turning a corner they came on a sight the Area Manager would never forget. In the middle of the store floor, where all the aisles converged like a town square, was a raised platform, about twenty feet across, covered with carpet. In the center of the platform sat a large executive desk. There was no doubt who sat behind the desk. A large sign proclaimed:

```
┌─────────────────────────────────────┐
│ ┌─────────────────────────────────┐ │
│ │                                 │ │
│ │          LEO VARLEY             │ │
│ │        MAY I HELP YOU?          │ │
│ │  PLEASE COME UP AND SAY HELLO.  │ │
│ │                                 │ │
│ └─────────────────────────────────┘ │
└─────────────────────────────────────┘
```

Charlie, with the Area Manager close behind, walked right up to the desk.

"Ah. There you are, Charles," Leo Varley said, looking up from his papers. "And this must be the friend you were telling me about. Do sit down. Welcome to Varley's."

Introductions over, the Area Manager couldn't help but ask about Leo's office. "Is this the first secret of creating Raving Fans?"

"Not exactly," laughed Leo. "But in my case it's certainly part of it. When our store moved into this mall I worried that I'd never get out of the office. I solved that by putting it right out here in the middle of things. Best move I ever made."

Charlie spoke up. "Our friend was wondering how you can afford to give away carnations, have play areas and fancy washrooms, and on top of that send people out of the store to buy things for customers elsewhere?"

"Wrong question," replied Leo firmly.

"Wrong question?" puzzled the Area Manager.

"Absolutely wrong question," confirmed Leo. "The real question is 'How can I afford *not* to do it?' This is Varley's and at Varley's Department Store we live the vision. The vision says, 'Carnations and make it a joy to shop here.' It doesn't say, 'No flowers, sorry we can't help you, and don't come shopping if you've got children.' "

"Glad to see you're sticking with the vision," said Charlie.

"Have to. It's what I want," replied Leo. Then, turning to the Area Manager, he said, "I understand you're interested in learning the first secret of creating Raving Fans?"

"I am," the Area Manager replied simply.

"Easy enough to do," said Leo, reaching into a drawer and lifting out a jewelry case. Opening the case, he took out a gold bracelet with a shield in the center.

"This is the Raving Fans bracelet. The first secret is engraved on it. When Charles taught me the Raving Fans secrets I volunteered to present each new candidate with a gold bracelet. Your wrist, please."

The Area Manager stretched his arm out across the desk and Leo snapped the bracelet in place.

Leo said, "Read what's engraved on the shield."

Turning the shield up to catch the light the Area Manager read:

The Area Manager was disappointed with the message. He had expected something more magical perhaps.

"You're wondering what it's all about, aren't you?" asked Leo.

"I am," the Area Manager replied honestly.

"I'd love to tell you all about the secret but Charles has a system for teaching the secrets and we know enough to follow systems, don't we, Charles?"

"Right you are, Leo. Systems are beautiful."

"So there we are," said Leo. "We'd best follow the system. But in the meantime I can tell you that the first thing you have to do is just what the shield says: **Decide what you want.** Remember, you are the source," concluded Leo.

"Time to go," sang out Charlie. "We've got a book being gift wrapped in the book department and then we're on our way to buy groceries."

With that, Charlie hustled the Area Manager off
the platform amid hurried good-byes. Charlie did
pause a moment, however, to ask, "I don't suppose
you've taken up golf?"

"Never touch it," replied Leo with a grin. "It's
addictive, I hear."

"Ah, well," said Charlie.

When they returned to the book department, the
Area Manager found his book gift wrapped, and as
Charlie had predicted, the price was exactly what
Varley's had paid.

"Thanks for all your help," said the Area
Manager to Linda. Then, leaning slightly forward, he
asked in a very serious manner, "Tell me, why do you
go to all this trouble?"

Linda answered with equal seriousness. "Well, it's store policy to look after customers' needs whenever possible. Mr. Varley calls it Raving Fan Service and he encourages us to use our own initiative. Besides, it's fun. I used to work in another department store. It was boring work. I resented the store treating me like a stupid machine, and my bad attitude was reflected in the way I treated their customers. It's the exact opposite at Varley's. Now I help people and enjoy doing it.

"I also like the feedback we get from our supervisors. We are all graded on our service to customers. The last store I worked in had mystery shoppers, but there the only feedback employees received was being dumped on by management if you didn't do well. Here management congratulates us when we do well and helps us when we don't. Raises and promotions go to those who deliver Raving Fan Service. It's nice to do a good job and be recognized for it."

The Area Manager thanked her again before saying good-bye.

On their way out the Area Manager noticed a sign by the ladies' dressing rooms that said, NO LIMIT ON CLOTHES TAKEN INTO THE DRESSING ROOMS: OUR STAFF WILL BE GLAD TO GO LOOK FOR OTHER COLORS OR SIZES OR BRING CLOTHING SUGGESTIONS TO YOU.

"Look at that sign," he said to Charlie. "I'll have to bring my wife here. It's worth the ride. She gets angry trying on outfits two or three pieces at a time and then having to go out of the changing room to exchange something."

"One customer out of a thousand steals something in a dressing room," said Charlie. "Next day the store puts up a sign offending the other nine hundred and ninety-nine customers and making one crook laugh as she finds a new way to steal. No one ever seems to compute the cost of offending so many customers in order to slow down one crook. Dressing-room limits are a blatant example of abusing customers. Now, think about the first secret and we'll head to our next appointment."

Charlie had told Leo Varley they were off to do their grocery shopping, and sure enough, after following Charlie's directions the Area Manager found himself turning in to Sally's Market. THE WORLD'S BEST GROCERY STORE was emblazoned on the side of the building.

Pulling into the parking lot the Area Manager noticed that huge pots filled with flowers marked each parking aisle while directly in front of his car was a valet parking booth. LET US PARK YOUR CAR. NO SENSE WASTING TIME PARKING WHEN YOU COULD BE SHOPPING AT SALLY'S a sign on the booth proclaimed. As he rolled to a stop by the booth an attendant in a bright kelly-green uniform opened his door.

"Welcome to Sally's Market," the attendant said cheerfully. "I'll park your car for you. Here's your claim check and a list of our specials today. If you like fresh strawberries I recommend ours. We brought in a truckload direct from the field so they could ripen on the vine rather than in a warehouse. I had some for lunch today. They were great."

The Area Manager had never been greeted like that at any grocery store or given a list of specials, along with a gentle sales pitch, before he was even out of his car.

While this was the Area Manager's first visit to Sally's, he had heard of the store before. A neighbor came weekly. He remembered suggesting to his wife that the neighbor must be crazy to drive forty miles, the distance from home, just to grocery shop. Already he was beginning to understand why she did it.

A red carpet extended from the valet parking booth to the store entrance. "I want to get some of those strawberries," he said to Charlie as they walked into the store. "That attendant certainly knew how to sell me. I love fresh strawberries."

"Most everybody loves fresh strawberries," Charlie pointed out. "Not much sense in greeting customers and bragging about broccoli or turnips. Now let's get a cart and go shopping. You've got your list."

Until that moment the Area Manager had forgotten his wife was working late and he had volunteered to grocery shop on the way home. "Thanks for reminding me, Charlie," he said as he dug the list out of his pocket and set off to fetch a shopping cart.

The store looked like an appealing place to shop. The aisles were wide, carpeted, and brightly lit. Although the store was obviously busy, it wasn't crowded.

"Looking good," thought the Area Manager to himself. "Two in a row, I bet. First Varley's, now this. Charlie just might know something about customer service after all."

"Of course I do," said Charlie with evident annoyance. "Now, go get your shopping done."

At that moment the Area Manager's attention was diverted. "Good afternoon, sir," said a young lady at his side. "I'm Judy and I'll be your store adviser this afternoon. I take it from your puzzled look this is your first visit to Sally's?"

"It is," admitted the Area Manager.

"That's great," said the adviser with obvious pleasure. "It's always fun to work with someone the first time. Of course, you are perfectly free to shop on your own, but my job is to help you get the best value and make your shopping as easy as possible. Do you have a list?"

"I do," said the Area Manager.

"Well, if you just take a seat at my desk here, I'm sure I can save you some money and some time," Judy said with a smile, gesturing to a row of small neat desks, each with a computer terminal on top.

The Area Manager started over to Judy's desk and turned to say something to Charlie but Charlie wasn't there! He spotted him seated by the door having his shoes shined. The sign above read: MAY WE POLISH YOUR SHOES? Under that, in large bold letters was the word: FREE.

"I bet shoeshines are popular," the Area Manager said to Judy as he sat down.

"That was Debbie's idea," replied Judy. "Most of our shoppers are women but often husbands come along to help, so Debbie suggested we give them a gift. And you're right. It's been popular. So popular, in fact, Debbie was promoted from stock clerk to cashier. Of course, she was providing Raving Fan Service on the floor too. You have to at Sally's, or you don't get promoted.

"Now, if you read me your list, I'll punch it into the computer and we'll see what we've got. I've memorized the code number for most items in the store, so you can read the list fairly fast."

The Area Manager took her at her word and Judy's fingers seemed to fly over the keypad as she entered each item. "That's it," said the Area Manager as he read off the last item. Beside Judy a printer presented his list.

"Let's have a look," said Judy as she slid the printed list across the desk and turned it around so he could read it. Using a pencil as a pointer she explained, "To start with, the computer has reorganized your list. If you follow the yellow arrows woven into the carpet, the items you pass first are at the top of the list and so on to the end. Next to each item is a recommended best buy. When you gave me a brand name it shows, along with the cost per unit, or per ounce, and if that's not our best-buy item, the list gives you a comparison."

"I see that," said the Area Manager as he studied the list. "But what are these items with a star?"

"Those are sale items not on your list. As you go along the stars will alert you to good deals."

"Like strawberries?" asked the Area Manager with a smile.

"Absolutely like strawberries," said Judy, pointing to one of the stars on the list. Then, moving her pencil across to the right-hand side of the list, she added, "The stars on this side alert you to items with excellent nutritional value. If there are any squares—here's one beside margarine—they warn you of items with little or no nutritional value or high fat content. The number here, on the far right, shows the grams of fat and the percentage of calories coming from that fat. The Heart Association and the Cancer Society both recommend that overall you keep fat calories to less than thirty percent of the total calories in your diet."

"Wow, I can see why there's a square opposite the margarine," exclaimed the Area Manager as he discovered 100 percent of the calories came from fat.

"Yes, it's got about the same nutritional value as engine oil," laughed Judy, "but I still like some on popcorn."

As the Area Manager stood up to begin shopping, he asked, "Do most of your customers use this service?"

"About twenty-five percent, I'd say," replied Judy. "The longer the shopping list they have, the more likely they are to get our help. Those that use us, though, really like it.

"Some of our customers prefer to enter their list themselves. That's what those computer terminals over there are for," she said, pointing to several computer screens and keyboards near the entrance.

"Now look at your list again," she continued. "That bar code at the bottom will be read by the cash register when you leave and alert our computer that we have a new customer. Our computer will then set up a customer record account for you and keep track of your purchases every time you shop here. Soon I'll be able to alert you to when your favorite brands are on sale, even though they might not be on your list.

"One more thing. If you wish, you can use our automated billing system."

"Automated billing system?" puzzled the Area Manager.

"Right," replied Judy. "On all package goods you'll find a bar-code tag like this," she continued, showing the Area Manager a one-inch-square piece of thin cardboard. "Just peel it off—it comes up easily— and drop it faceup in the tray on the side of the cart. When you leave, the cashier will slide the tags into a special bar-code reader. In a few seconds all your package goods will be totaled up."

"That sounds great," said the Area Manager with obvious approval.

"It works well and the customers like it," said Judy. "Next month we will be able to weigh and measure produce purchases right in the produce department and give you a tag there too."

"Do you run spot checks to make sure customers are honest? Seems to me they could pocket a tag," wondered the Area Manager.

"When we bag your order we pass several items over a bar-code scanner to ensure they match up. We don't do it to catch dishonest customers, though," replied Judy. "We know our loss—what we call shrinkage—is far below the average for this industry. Our customers are honest. We run the random sample to ensure the equipment is working properly. That's a comfort both to us and to the customers."

"Good idea," agreed the Area Manager.

"We think so," laughed Judy. "Now, if you have any questions as you shop, every department has a manager on the floor. They're there to help."

"Thank you very much," said the Area Manager with genuine appreciation as he headed off for the first aisle with his new list.

"I see you've met a store adviser," said Charlie as he joined him.

"And you've had your shoes polished," observed the Area Manager.

"Looking great," said Charlie, pointing down with pleasure at his gleaming shoes. Then he added, "Let's shop."

"After you, twinkle toes," laughed the Area Manager as he and Charlie headed off down the first aisle.

The shopping was soon finished and the Area Manager found himself at the checkout stand. The computerized list had been a real help. Several times he had chosen a healthy alternative, thanks to a fat-content alert, and he had picked up two other specials as well as the strawberries. The automated checkout worked well and was fast. There were no lines at the checkout stands.

As he began to push his cart to the door he heard a sudden cry of delight. Turning, he saw a lady wearing a kelly-green uniform jacket bounding toward them. She crossed the floor in three strides and threw her arms around Charlie.

"Charlie, you old Fairy Godmother. Where have you been? Good to see you. What's up? Come on into the office!" All the words came rushing out at once.

"George, look after this cart and bring us some coffee, will you?" Sally called out as she ushered them into her office. "Best waiter I've got," she added with a mischievous smile.

"Don't believe her," said Charlie. "George is her brother. They've been teasing each other since day one."

George entered with a pot of coffee and a sheaf of paper cups. "Here is your coffee, madam," he said with a smile. "I'll help bag groceries while you play the grand lady of customer service." So saying, George whipped off his cap with a flourish and backed out the door bowing.

As he watched Sally and her brother the Area Manager was beginning to wonder what was going on. It didn't seem very businesslike to him. Nor for that matter did Leo's desk arrangement.

"No, it's not," he heard Charlie's quiet voice beside him say. "On the other hand, businesslike businesses, as you call them, aren't necessarily famous for customer service either. Varley's and Sally's Market are."

The Area Manager smiled at Charlie to acknowledge the point and turning to Sally said, "You obviously know Charlie."

"Good heavens, yes," laughed Sally. "Charlie rescued me from certain bankruptcy about eight years ago. He's the best Fairy Godmother a girl ever had."

"He's your Fairy Godmother?"

"For eight years now. It takes some getting used to, doesn't it?"

"It certainly does," agreed the Area Manager.

"Don't worry. It will come," said Sally. Turning to Charlie she said, "I take it our friend has been to see Leo and I'm to tell him how the first secret of creating Raving Fans works?"

"As always," agreed Charlie.

"You've done this before?" the Area Manager asked Sally.

"Oh, yes, many times, but not half often enough. Everybody has a Fairy Godmother but they don't show up on a whim. You have to need them and accept them."

"Tell me. Is Charlie Leo's Fairy Godmother too?" asked the Area Manager.

"Of course," replied Sally. "Leo is a believer. And he knows he needs help. Trouble is, most people don't believe they need help. They don't really care about customers. If you don't care about customers, you don't get to meet your Fairy Godmother—at least if Charlie's your Fairy Godmother you don't."

"Well, I care," said the Area Manager. "At least I think I do. But the problem is, I really don't know anything about satisfying customers."

At that, Charlie let out a groan and rolled his eyes skyward.

"I mean about creating Raving Fans," the Area Manager corrected himself. "Satisfied customers just aren't good enough, are they, Charlie?"

"I'm mollified if not impressed," grumped Charlie.

"Don't mind him," Sally said to the Area Manager with a friendly smile. "He arrived one day with another Godmother who told me he's been in a blue funk about customer service for nearly a century now. But he really is a dear. Aren't you, Charlie?"

The Area Manager could have sworn he saw Charlie blush.

Sally continued, "Drink your coffee and think about golf. I've got work to do with our new friend."

The Area Manager smiled and looked at Sally expectantly.

"You know the first magic secret is **Decide What You Want.** Are you ready to learn what to do with it?"

"I am," the Area Manager replied eagerly.

"When you decide what you want you must— **create a vision of perfection centered on the customer.**"

The Area Manager repeated slowly, "Create a vision of perfection."

"Right. You're the source. It's what you want as perfection that comes first," said Sally. "Take note that the secret doesn't say you have to be perfect. It tells you to imagine perfection centered on the customer."

"Well, I guess I can imagine anything, but I've got to tell you this vision business sounds a little off the wall to me," said the Area Manager dubiously.

"It may sound that way," said Sally, "but it is probably the best hard-nosed business advice you'll ever hear."

"That's quite a statement," laughed the Area Manager. "Tell me more."

"Let me tell you about my own experience," Sally said. "I bought this grocery store a year before Charlie showed up. I had a huge mortgage and was headed down the bankruptcy drain.

"I was trying to sell produce that some days was hardly fit for the compost heap. I didn't believe I could afford to throw it out. I was ashamed of my store and I knew I had to treat my customers better if I was going to succeed. But I didn't know how to do it. Then Charlie showed up.

"When I learned the first secret of creating Raving Fans, I decided what I wanted. Then I went off by myself and in my mind's eye I began to paint what the perfect grocery market would look like. I pictured exactly how the store would serve the customer. It took some time, but I worked it all out. I could see every detail just by closing my eyes.

"I knew precisely what happened to customers. I could see them arrive. I could picture the valet parking and someone to tell them about a wonderful special. I saw store advisers and computers helping people make the best choices to save money and eat a healthy diet. I saw a manager for each department always on the floor to help customers and make sure their area was perfect. I could see natural lighting in the fruit and vegetable section so people could really see what color the food was. I saw the assistance program, where young people are available to take elderly shoppers around the store to read small print on labels and lift heavier items. I saw carpet on the floor and automatic checkout stands. Lots of checkout stands so no one had to wait in a long line. Imagine. Stores making customers line up to pay the store money! Not at Sally's, I can tell you!

"It was all here in my head. It was a fantasy and it was perfect. Every detail was so clear in my mind that I felt as if I could reach out and touch it. It was what I wanted. I was the source."

"That's some vision," said the Area Manager with obvious respect.

"It was bound to be. I created the best grocery market, where anything is possible—in my head. That vision is always in my mind. I know exactly what perfection looks like so I know what my goal is.

"Once you have a real vision, what you have to do is bring down the picture from your mind and impose it over your organization and see where the bumps and warts are. That's what you work on."

Sally turned to Charlie, "How did I do, Coach? Or are you off on a golf course somewhere?"

"You did fine, Sally. Just fine," said Charlie.

The Area Manager suddenly felt convinced that he had been told a secret that had obviously worked for Leo and Sally and that could work for him. "So, once I have my vision, and I compare it to the way things actually are, what do I do next?" he asked with excitement.

"First you need a vision," said Charlie. "Let's go. Time for Sally to go back to work."

As they said good-bye, Sally invited the Area
Manager to visit again, anytime. "I'd be glad to help
in any way I can."

Charlie and the Area Manager reclaimed their
grocery bags and cart and headed for the parking lot.
Soon their car was brought around; they loaded the
bags into the backseat and headed home. The Area
Manager was impressed with Sally's Market. "I've
done a lot of grocery shopping," he told Charlie, "but
never has it been so easy and enjoyable. I saved
money too. Those sale items were a real buy. Maybe
I've become a Raving Fan," he said with a broad grin.

"Naturally," said Charlie. "Now I want you to
spend some time thinking about *your* company and
what *you* want."

"Sure thing," said the Area Manager
enthusiastically. "Then will I learn the second secret?"

"We'll see," said Charlie with a laugh. Then
much more seriously. "I'll give you a call in a couple
of days. Let's have a game of golf."

The Area Manager was about to reply when he realized Charlie was no longer seated beside him. The shock of losing Charlie was worse than the shock of finding him.

"I've lost him," he anguished.

"Not unless you give up golf," he heard Charlie's voice say. "Matter of fact, not even then. Fairy Godmothers are always around when you need them. Don't worry. I'll call."

A great calm settled over the Area Manager as he drove home that night. His wife was surprised to find he had driven forty miles to Sally's market but delighted with the shopping and fresh produce. The Area Manager just smiled when she wondered why he had gone all the way to Sally's. He wasn't ready to tell anyone about Charlie just yet. He needed some time to believe himself what had happened.

The next few days at the office were unusually productive. In his own mind he was focusing on when customers used his company's product. While he was a long way from painting the perfect picture, he was miles ahead of where he had been in knowing what his customer-service goal was going to be.

He also knew that he had to create Raving Fans. Satisfied customers just weren't good enough. He knew the first secret: **DECIDE WHAT YOU WANT.** Next, he knew, he had to create a vision of perfection centered on when the customer used the product. Finally, to check out how he was doing, he knew he had to bring the vision of perfection down to the level of what was actually happening and then see where the bumps and warts were.

One morning several days later, the Area Manager answered his phone to hear a familiar voice. "How's chances for a game of golf?"

He quickly agreed. "I'll pick you up at noon then," Charlie said. "Be at the front door. My turn to drive."

Promptly at noon the Area Manager was waiting for Charlie.

"We'll have to skip golf for now," said Charlie as the Area Manager got in the car. "Too much to do. Sorry about that. But all play and no work makes Charlie a failed Fairy Godmother."

The Area Manager was no longer surprised at anything Charlie might do or say. He also knew there was no sense wondering about the second secret or where they were going until Charlie was ready to tell him.

He didn't have long to wonder. Soon Charlie parked in front of a manufacturing plant. Inside the lobby the Area Manager discovered numerous plaques and award certificates. They were all from customers and they all praised the plant for such things as quality or on-time delivery. Several were Supplier of the Year awards.

A few minutes later the Area Manager found himself meeting Bill, the plant's manager, in his office.

He wasn't surprised to find that Charlie was also Bill's Fairy Godmother. But he was surprised to find that Bill, the manager of a huge plant for a large national company, admitted so readily to having a Fairy Godmother.

"He's wondering how you can be so matter-of-fact about having a Fairy Godmother," Charlie announced to Bill, again demonstrating his disconcerting ability to pick up thoughts.

"Well I don't broadcast it in public," Bill confessed with a smile. "But I know you wouldn't be here if you didn't have the capacity and willingness to believe. So tell me, what have you learned so far?"

"I learned from Charlie that to succeed I need to create Raving Fans. Satisfied customers just aren't good enough.

"I also learned that I have to decide what I want and then create a vision of perfection centered on the moment the customer uses the product," said the Area Manager. "If you're willing to teach me, I think I'm ready to learn the second secret of creating Raving Fans."

"It certainly sounds like you're ready," agreed Bill.

"The second secret is the market secret. Turn over the shield on your bracelet and read what it says."

He was sure the shield was blank on the second face when Leo gave it to him, but when he looked he now found the second secret:

Discover What
the Customer
Wants

The Area Manager read the message. Again he was a little disappointed. The secret seemed somewhat obvious.

"Bill, enlighten my friend," said Charlie. "Tell him how the second secret works."

"Delighted," agreed Bill. "All you need to do is discover the customers' vision of what they really want and then alter your vision if need be."

"Hold on," said the Area Manager. "If what the customer wants is to be the same as what I want, why did I bother having a vision in the first place?"

"Good question. Three things to learn," said Bill.

"First, unless you have your own vision, how can you understand the customers'? Imagine opening a hamburger restaurant dedicated to producing the world's best hamburger and then trying to discuss with a customer your bacon cheeseburger without first working out what you thought that bacon cheeseburger should be. You would have a tough time communicating! The customer says it should have Roquefort cheese and an onion croissant for the bun. What do you say if you don't have any idea what you think a perfect bacon cheeseburger is? A customer's vision has meaning only in the context of your vision.

"Second, when you find out what customers really want, what their vision is, it will likely focus on just one or two things. Your own vision has to fill in the gaps.

"Finally, you have to know when to ignore what the customer wants and, if necessary, tell the customer to take his vision elsewhere to be fulfilled," Bill concluded.

Telling a customer to take his vision elsewhere struck the Area Manager as pure heresy. "I mean, you just don't tell customers to take a hike," he protested.

"You don't unless their vision is so different from yours that no fit is possible."

"This is the Raving Fan class, isn't it?" the Area Manager asked plaintively. "If I go back and start telling customers to go elsewhere, I'm going to need more than a Fairy Godmother to save me."

"You'll soon be able to save yourself," Charlie assured him. "Tell the man how the rest of it works," he said to Bill.

"The issue isn't telling customers to take a hike, although that might happen. The point is that customer service is as much a part of your product as any screw or bolt.

"No one would dream of trying to design and market a sports car that was also a great off-road vehicle and at the same time served as a commercial delivery van. Yet when it comes to customer service, those who decide to really try to give good service often aim to be everything to everybody. That doesn't work," said Bill.

"I must admit I thought good customer service meant looking after every whim of the customer," said the Area Manager.

"Only within the window you've defined in your vision as your particular customer service product," responded Bill. "I understand you were over to see Sally. Did her staff help you load the groceries into your car?"

"Come to think of it, they didn't. Where we usually shop, they do. That's interesting."

"You were likely impressed by what Sally did offer because within her customer service window she strives to be the world's best. But if you think about it, there's lots she doesn't do," said Bill.

"For example, she doesn't have rug-cleaning machines for rent, she doesn't sell fresh fish, and she won't develop camera film for you. Those services are all offered by some grocery stores but not by Sally, and yet her customers say she has better service than any other grocery store in town. If you want those services though, you have to go elsewhere. They are not part of her vision. In essence she says 'Take a hike.' "

"You might think her vision is deficient," commented Charlie, "but she constantly strives to improve what she has decided to achieve. As long as customers are pouring through the grocery store all day long, her vision isn't deficient. Not by a long shot."

The Area Manager sat quietly for a minute. As he thought about it, he had to agree that those businesses he would call service leaders performed within a well-defined window. There were lots of things they could do but didn't.

"So that's why I first have to have the vision myself. So I know what my window of customer service is?" he said.

"The customer's vision might change your window, but if you don't have your own vision to start with, you'll never put the necessary limits in place," said Bill.

Charlie, who had been following the conversation with interest, agreed and then added, "Remember Bill's first two points. Having your own vision before you talk to customers also puts you in a position where you can understand the customer's vision. It also allows you to fill in the gaps between your vision and their vision, so you have a complete picture."

"Well then, how do I go about finding out what my customers' vision is?" questioned the Area Manager.

"Good question," said Bill. "At this company we use a very sophisticated technique Charlie taught me many years ago."

Again the Area Manager leaned forward to catch Bill's words of wisdom. "Yes?" he prompted.

"We ask them," Bill replied.

"Ask them?" said the Area Manager. "You ask them?"

"Isn't it a wonderful idea?" said Bill enthusiastically. "It works like a charm. We ask them and then we listen closely both to what they say and to what they don't say. But first you have to discover who your customers are."

"Discover who your customers are?" wondered the Area Manager.

"Right. Take this plant as an example. Tell me. What do you know about our business?"

"Not a thing really," admitted the Area Manager.

"Here's a quick lesson then. We manufacture metal parts that other manufacturers then incorporate into their products. For example, we make metal cases for a computer company. Now who is our customer?" asked Bill.

"I'd say the computer company, but it's too obvious an answer," replied the Area Manager.

"You're right. Tell me who at that company would be our customer?"

"I guess your real customer is the buyer. The purchasing agent," said the Area Manager.

"Good start," agreed Bill. "But everyone touched by the product is a customer. What about the engineering department that always wants to make changes in the product? And what about the production department that has to use the cases?"

"You're right. You've got three customers. Buyers, engineering, and operations," the Area Manager said.

"Three! If life were only so simple. What about the receiver who gets the cases on his loading dock? If you ship on pallets that are difficult for his forklift to handle, guess whose shipment gets left on the loading dock? Then there's the accounting department that needs a special tax number on each invoice or they won't process it for payment. That's a customer whose vision is important too!"

"That's a lot of customers," said the Area Manager.

"It's getting there. Next add on the owner of the computer company, who has his own ideas. Then there is the quality control department that delights in scratching the finish with pocket knives to see how well the paint is baked on. It does begin to add up," said Bill, shaking his head with wonder. "They are all touched by our product and they're all customers."

"The people who ultimately buy and use the computer must be customers too," suggested the Area Manager.

"I'll tell the world," agreed Bill. "We'd better be sure to have a finish on our cases that can withstand coffee spills.

"Everyone from the original purchasing agent to the end user is a customer and your vision had better include every single one of them or you'll never create Raving Fans."

The Area Manager said he now understood that just knowing who the customer was could be complicated.

"It is, but discovering exactly what the customer wants can be difficult too," said Bill.

"So what's your secret of success?" asked the Area Manager.

"It's a matter of training your ear," answered Bill. "First, you have to listen to the music as well as the lyrics. Often what people really want doesn't show up directly in what they say. They may even say one thing and mean quite another."

"Like what?" asked the Area Manager.

"Like the purchasing agent who tells you the only thing they look at is price and so you had best sharpen your pencil, but actually the real priorities are quality and on-time delivery. Like the owner of the computer company who says he wants a case with a unique look, but what he really wants is something as close as he can get to the encasement of the best-selling computer—without being taken to court. That's what I mean by listening to the music as well as to the lyrics."

The Area Manager nodded his head. "I understand now what you mean. I've seen it happen myself, but when I've discovered the customers' music and lyrics were different, it's usually been too late. I'll be more alert and watch for that in the future," he promised.

"There's more," continued Bill. "Next, you need to learn about the two traps of customer listening."

"Two traps?" queried the Area Manager.

"Well, there are really three," laughed Bill, "but I've already told you about the first one: customers saying one thing and meaning another. That leaves two: 'Fine' and silence."

"Where do we start?" asked the Area Manager.

"With silence," replied Bill. "Tell me, have you had any bad customer service experiences lately?"

"Does Charlie like golf?" replied the Area Manager with a laugh. "Would you like to hear about the rotten service and cold dinner I had last week?"

"What I'd really like to hear is what you did."

"I ate the cold dinner. I was hungry," said the Area Manager.

"Did you complain? Demand to see the manager?"

"No, I didn't. I was so fed up I didn't even fill out the customer service card that was on the table."

"I react the same way," said Bill. "I never fill out those cards when I'm unhappy and I rarely complain to management. Why don't I complain? Simple. I don't believe it does any good."

"You're darn tootin' it doesn't do any good," said the Area Manager. "Waste of time and a waste of ink. I bet that restaurant wouldn't even read the card, much less do anything about it. If they did care, they wouldn't have cold food to begin with!"

"Let that be a lesson to you, then," exclaimed Bill.

"A lesson to me?" said a perplexed Area Manager.

"Yes, you. Learn that silence is a message and usually it's not a good one."

"Ah. I see what you're getting at," said the Area Manager.

"Next lesson then. I'll stick with restaurants. Even worse than silence, how often have you left a restaurant where there was a problem with the meal or the service and when the hostess at the door asks how everything was you say 'Fine'?"

The Area Manager smiled and nodded his head. "You're right. I almost always say 'Fine.' "

"Exactly. Past experience has taught us people don't care—or they don't want to make a fuss—so why bother? Customers assume no one really wants to know what they think," said Bill.

"You're dead right," said the Area Manager. "Last week we received a shipment of supplies that was two weeks late. Before we even opened the boxes I knew our quality-control department would reject about eight percent. The salesman who looks after our account was in to see me yesterday and I didn't complain. I don't think our supplier cares much. But I should have said something. If our customers treat us the same way I treat our suppliers, we'll never get any feedback."

"You've got it," said Bill. "When a customer complains, you know you're hearing the truth. Listen to him. When a customer is a Raving Fan and is enthusiastic, listen to him too. But when a customer is silent or says 'Fine' with a smile, you have to really perk up your ears. You've got a problem. If nothing else, that customer isn't a Raving Fan."

"What you're saying," said the Area Manager, "is that I've got to listen hardest when the customer isn't talking."

"You've got to listen hard all the time. Just don't lighten up when the customer smiles and says 'Fine' or if the message is silence," replied Bill.

"So how do you listen to silence?" asked the Area Manager.

"Well, to start with, you recognize that 'Fine' or silence is a message in itself and you start asking more questions. Sincere questions."

"Sincere questions?"

"Of course," said Bill. "Remember, past experience has taught customers that chances are you don't really want to know what they think and feel. If they are going to open up you have to first gain credibility."

"I guess that can be tough to do," observed the Area Manager.

"It can take a while," agreed Bill. "But if you take the time to get a conversation going, customers will sense you're serious and will respond. The first thing, though, is to know enough to realize that 'Fine' or silence is an important message."

At that moment the Area Manager happened to look out the window of Bill's office. The sky had clouded over and it had started to rain.

"Good thing we didn't go golfing after all, Charlie," he said. "That rain wasn't forecast."

"No reason not to keep hard at work," said Charlie.

"Just in case it clears up and there is time for a round of golf later?" Bill suggested with a knowing smile.

"Well," replied Charlie, lapsing into a mischievous grin, "it would be foolish to waste the sun that is due back in forty-seven minutes. I suggest we hurry on. It will take us a good thirty minutes to get to the golf course from here."

"I'm glad we're nearly finished," Bill said to the Area Manager. "Keeping Charlie from the first tee requires a man braver than I am."

"Braver than me too," laughed the Area Manager. "But before Charlie and I play golf, tell me, once I've listened to the customers and discovered their vision, how do I fit that together with my vision? Seems to me that could be pretty complex."

"Another good question and exactly the topic I want to discuss," said Bill. "You don't have two complete visions and then try to make one. It comes together bit by bit. You may have a pretty good idea of your own vision, but you'll likely only discover the customers' in small nuggets. These you fit into your vision or reject.

"For example, when I took on this plant I had a vision of what I thought perfection was. I could close my eyes, lean back, and walk around in my mind. I created a movie in my head and I actually felt I could step in, walk around, and see what was happening. Customers weren't just buying the product, they were coming to us with problems, and our team was finding solutions for them where our competition had failed. Instead of just suggesting improvements or doing a drawing, we surprised them by making prototypes to show exactly what we could do.

"I had a pretty complete vision before I started to talk to customers. Then I found out that customers didn't have complete visions. A lot of them were just zeroed in on two or three things. One customer I remember was a fanatic about the way we painted his product."

"So all he cared about was painting?" questioned the Area Manager.

"It wasn't all he cared about, but that was his focus. He just didn't worry about the rest. He is quite typical. Most customers have a focus. You have to find that focus and then mine it for information. As you uncover the customer's vision one bit at a time, it's easy to either work it into your own vision or reject it."

The Area Manager nodded his head in understanding. "Come to think of it, I know exactly what you mean by customers having a narrow focus of what they want. My seven-year-old son didn't like the macaroni and cheese at the hotel we stayed at last summer. Noticing this problem, our waiter told him, 'If you come back for dinner here tomorrow, I promise that I will have the same macaroni you have at home if your mom will just tell me how she makes it.'

"The next night the waiter greeted him with 'I have your macaroni and cheese for you tonight.' They had gone out and bought the same brand we eat at home. In fact, the waiter brought the box to show my son. That restaurant owner had happy children and parents in his customer service vision," concluded the Area Manager.

"Great story," said Bill. "It illustrates an interesting truth about customer visions. Often, the narrower the focus, the more important that vision is to the customer. If you want macaroni just the way Mom makes it at home, no compromise is acceptable."

"I'm beginning to appreciate the importance of the customer's vision even if it is narrow," said the Area Manager.

"The immediate vision may be narrow, but customers care about everything," said Charlie. "It's just that most of them haven't thought through their whole relationship with you, only some specific areas. Because customers are often so focused on a specific priority, it's easy to match up what they want with that area of your vision. But first you have to discover what they really want.

"And to discover what they really want you have to listen to the music as well as the lyrics. We're right back where we started. We've covered it all," added Charlie as his gaze drifted to the outside window where the rain had ended.

"And speaking of listening to the music, I hear the Eighteen-Hole Symphony playing. I think we have time for a game," Charlie said brightly. "If we're all finished here, we may as well be on our way."

Before they left, the Area Manager asked Bill one final question, "Tell me, do you somehow keep track of how you're doing with customer service and tie raises and promotions to that?"

"Of course," Bill replied. "We have a Raving Fan Index we measure monthly for every department and every person working here. We talk to customers and use internal benchmarks like re-work or on-time-delivery scores to put the index together. Everyone who works here knows who their customer is. Usually it's the next person in the chain to get their work, be it product or paper. But sometimes our people might have several customers, both internal and external. Their Raving Fan Index is tied directly to their own customer base and that counts heavily toward both raises and promotions."

"Interesting," said the Area Manager.

"And profitable for both the company and the workers," said Bill.

"If you don't look after your people, they won't look after your customers," said Charlie. "And when they do, if you say thank you and reward them, they'll do it again and again." Charlie paused and added in a firm voice, "It's called common sense."

Their business concluded, they departed. As they reached Charlie's car, the sun broke through the clouds. The Area Manager suggested that perhaps the reason they'd gone directly to see Bill was that Charlie had somehow known an unforecasted rain would be passing through. Charlie didn't reply but smiled and gave a slight shrug of protest as if to say, "Who? Me? How could you even think such a thing?"

They arrived at the golf club thirty minutes later and soon drove off from the first tee. No magic this time. Charlie's drive landed short of the green but the Area Manager landed in a sand trap halfway to the hole.

Charlie ignored customer service and concentrated on his golf game. This suited the Area Manager. He had learned a lot that afternoon and he was glad to have some quiet time to review it all in his mind and think how he could start finding out what his company's customers really wanted.

Already he had a couple of areas where he wanted to start improving service, but now he realized his priorities might not be the same as his customers' priorities. First he had to find ways of getting good feedback from customers and then he had to learn to listen to the music behind what they were saying.

When they left the golf club, Charlie instructed the Area Manager to again take a few days to work on what he had learned.

"When you think you're ready to learn the third secret, give me a call," said Charlie.

"A call? You have a phone number?"

"Don't bother with one. Just pick up the phone, and if you want me I'll be there."

"All right," agreed the Area Manager. "One final thing, though. Considering you're doing the driving, I trust your departure will be somewhat more conventional this time."

"I'll drop you off right where I found you," promised Charlie.

As he stood on the curb and watched Charlie pull away, the Area Manager realized the car and Charlie had disappeared. Not into the traffic but suddenly just not there. Equally amazing, no one else seemed to notice.

The Area Manager stared at the empty street, shaking his head and thinking, "It's something like going to a movie in which animated cartoon characters walk around with real people. When you're in the theater it's all perfectly reasonable, but afterward it's difficult to believe how real it seemed."

The next morning there was an envelope on the Area Manager's desk. Inside was a single sheet of paper. "Cartoon characters . . . real people! You owe me a golf game for that one, my friend. Call when you're ready. Charlie."

The Area Manager smiled to himself and punched the button on his intercom. "Leslie, please get hold of all the managers in my department and call a meeting for two P.M. The agenda will be one item: 'Talking to customers.' Thanks."

The next few days were busy and fun for the Area Manager as he began the task of turning his whole department into a customer-listening post. No Raving Fans were discovered, but only 3 percent of customers contacted had a negative comment about the company or its service.

"Seems to me we're doing pretty good," his Sales Manager suggested.

"I think you're wrong on that," the Area Manager replied. "We haven't uncovered a single Raving Fan. Perhaps ninety-seven percent of our customers are so fed up they can't even be bothered to complain and tell us where we're going wrong. I told you before, we have to learn to listen to the music as well as to the lyrics. All I hear is the thundering applause of one hand clapping."

"One hand clapping?" puzzled the Sales Manager.

"Right. One hand clapping and it looks like this," said the Area Manager, lifting his right arm and flapping his hand up and down like a child waving good-bye. "Those customers may be telling us they'll leave first chance they get." After a pause he concluded, "We've got big work ahead of us."

Several times the Area Manager was tempted to reach for the telephone and call Charlie, but he knew he already had more than he could handle with the first two secrets. He was starting to understand what his customers were thinking and he was beginning to filter this information into his own vision of perfection. Bit by bit he was beginning to feel confident enough to share some of the vision with his managers and he could see that they were becoming as excited as he was with the challenge.

He had been warned there would be differences between how he envisioned the customer using the product and how his customers would view the same event. Nevertheless, he was surprised to see how very different those visions were with some customers on a few key points.

He had also discovered some unhappy customers whose expectations were so far outside his window that he knew he could never satisfy their needs. The Area Manager realized some of these complainers were customers who should be told politely that what they wanted wasn't part of his company's customer service package. Rather than give them extra time and attention—further diverting his company from its true vision—he should suggest they look elsewhere.

As all this fell into place, the Area Manager began to feel he was still short a piece of the puzzle. The time had come, he decided, to call Charlie. The idea of just picking up the phone and finding Charlie at the other end seemed silly. He hoped Charlie might sense his need and again suddenly appear on the couch with golf clubs in hand. But no such luck. So, feeling foolish, the Area Manager decided to try what Charlie had suggested and he picked up the telephone. Just then it rang.

"Hello," he answered.

Charlie's voice came down the line. "I thought you'd never call. Perfect golf weather and you're so busy talking to customers you haven't had time for your old friends."

"You said to call when I was ready," the Area Manager answered defensively. "I haven't been ready."

"Fine way to treat a golfing buddy," huffed Charlie. "I never said we couldn't get in three or four games while you practiced listening to customers. Ah, well, there it is. We'll just have to make the best of it."

Then Charlie added in a much brighter tone, "Golf this afternoon, then?"

"Suits me," replied the Area Manager. "Do I pick you up or will you come by here?"

"I'll arrange a ride for you and meet you there. It's all part of learning the third magic secret," said Charlie.

"Tell me," he continued, "what do you know about the taxi service in this city?"

"Just what I've experienced myself or heard from friends," replied the Area Manager. "All the cab drivers seem to have a chip on their shoulder and the service . . ."

"... is awful," finished Charlie.

"You'll find your ride to the club an experience," said Charlie. "There'll be a taxi waiting for you out front at exactly twelve o'clock."

Precisely at noon the Area Manager was at the front door. There at the curb was his taxi. But the Area Manager noticed this taxi was not only clean, it was actually polished to a bright shine.

At that moment the driver's door opened and out sprang a middle-aged man in a white shirt, black tie, and freshly pressed gray slacks.

"Good afternoon," said the cabbie as he rounded the rear of the car and reached out to open the back passenger door. "I'm Dennis, your driver. You must be the person I'm to take to the golf club."

"Yes, I am," agreed the Area Manager as he got into the taxi and Dennis closed the door behind him.

The Area Manager saw the inside of the car matched the exterior. Spotlessly clean!

"I've got the air-conditioning on. Is it comfortable for you?" asked Dennis.

"Why, yes. Fine," said the surprised Area Manager.

"If you would like the radio, please let me know," continued Dennis. "I'd be glad to put on your favorite station. Or if you would rather have music, I have a library of tapes with everything from rock to classical."

"That's nice," responded the Area Manager, so taken aback he was unsure what else to say.

Starting the car and pulling away from the curb Dennis added, "In the seat pocket in front of you, you will find several magazines and today's paper. Up front I've a small cooler beside me and if you would like a soft drink I'd be glad to hand you a complimentary juice or cola. I also have a thermos of regular coffee and one of decaf if you'd rather have a cup of coffee."

The Area Manager thought he had landed on Mars. "I can see why Charlie said I'd enjoy *this* ride."

"I trust you will enjoy it," said Dennis. "At this time of day I think it will be fastest to go up the interstate and then across on Arnett Road if that suits you."

"Sounds good to me," said the Area Manager.

"Just one last thing. If you would like to talk I'd be glad to discuss most anything except religion or politics. If you prefer to just sit back and enjoy the ride I'll be quiet."

The Area Manager decided to talk. "Tell me, how long have you been serving your customers like this?"

"Since the great awakening," replied Dennis.

"The great awakening?" asked the Area Manager.

"Yup. The greatest awakening since the Prince kissed Snow White," said Dennis.

"What happened?"

"Well, I was sitting in a taxi line one day waiting for a fare, thinking how awful everything was and listening to the radio. The program host was interviewing an author named Wayne Dyer. He had just written a book called *You'll See It When You Believe It.* He said, 'If you get up in the morning expecting to have a bad day, you'll rarely disappoint yourself.' He went on to say, 'Stop complaining! Differentiate yourself from your competition. Don't be a duck. Be an eagle. Ducks quack and complain. Eagles soar above the crowd.'

"That hit me right between the eyes," said Dennis. "He was really talking about me. I was always complaining. Quack! Quack! Quack! So I decided to change my attitude and become an eagle. I looked around at the other cabs and their drivers. The cabs were dirty, the drivers were unfriendly, and the customers were unhappy. So I decided to make some changes."

"Was that tough?" asked the Area Manager.

"Not really," said Dennis as he turned the cab onto the interstate and headed toward the golf club. "I decided I was going to do it right and enjoy myself. One by one I started to make changes, beginning with cleaning up the car, installing a telephone, printing up a nice-looking calling card, and deciding that my customers were my number-one priority."

"I take it this has paid off for you?" asked the Area Manager.

"It sure has," said Dennis with a big grin.

"The first month it didn't make much difference, but I kept at it. Soon customers started to call and business picked up. I don't sit at cab stands anymore. I book appointments."

When they arrived at the golf club Dennis bounced out and opened the door for the Area Manager.

"It was a real pleasure to serve you, sir," he said, handing him a card. "Please call if I can ever be of service."

"One last thing," said the Area Manager.

"Yes, sir?"

"Why won't you discuss religion or politics?"

"Experience, just experience. Those are the two topics that upset customers. Upset customers are not happy customers and unhappy customers are not big tippers," replied Dennis with a broad smile as he touched his brow with the fingers of his right hand in a farewell salute.

Dennis pulled away and the Area Manager turned to find Charlie at his side.

"Well, what did you think of that ride?" Charlie asked.

"Quite simply, the most incredible taxi ride I've ever had," the Area Manager said with awe. "I never knew a taxi like that existed in this city."

"Sounds like you're a Raving Fan," said Charlie.

"Darn right I'm a Raving Fan. That guy Dennis is nothing short of a genius."

"I don't know about a genius, but he does know something about the third magic secret of creating Raving Fans," said Charlie. "Now, let's get down to the real business of living and play golf."

The Area Manager knew that once Charlie scented a golf game there would be no getting his attention onto creating Raving Fans for any longer than sixty seconds until the last putt dropped into the 18th hole, so he readily agreed.

When the game was over, Charlie invited the Area Manager for a ride. "Let's see what we can discover about this third magic secret."

Once on the interstate Charlie told the Area Manager to close his eyes and think about the vision he had now created with the help of his customers.

"I want you to promise me to keep your eyes closed until I tell you to open them. All right?"

Puzzled, but trusting Charlie, the Area Manager closed his eyes and called to mind his vision. He was lost in his thoughts when Charlie spoke again.

"When I tell you to open your eyes, don't be surprised to find that we're on a different road," said Charlie. "Okay. Open."

"I'm not surprised. I'm astounded," said the Area Manager discovering huge pine trees alongside the road. "Where are we?"

Charlie named a state more than halfway across the country.

"Surprised? Why should I be surprised?" the Area Manager muttered helplessly, shaking his head in bewilderment. "I suppose you always like to drop in here on your way home from golf."

"Sometimes I do," laughed Charlie. "Mostly though, I come to show off what you're about to see. If I could show you anything like this close to home, I would. Unfortunately, examples of true Raving Fan Service are few and far between."

The Area Manager was about to ask Charlie how he had accomplished such a neat bit of travel, but decided he really didn't want to know. He was here. He was safe. And, he consoled himself, he was going to see another example of Raving Fan Service and learn the third magic secret of creating Raving Fans.

"Glad to see you adapting so well to the trip," said Charlie. "First time through it's always an experience. But now, if you feel ready, let's get started on the third secret."

The Area Manager said he was as ready as he'd ever be.

"Great. Watch this," said Charlie as he pulled into a gasoline station beside the road. "Here it comes—the third secret in action."

Before the car came to a stop at the pumps, two attendants in bright-red jumpsuits burst from the service-station office and ran over to greet them. As they approached the car, the Area Manager saw that both were well groomed and their uniforms were spotless.

Charlie's car rolled to a stop as one began cleaning the windows while the other appeared at the driver's window, smiling with such enthusiasm that the Area Manager couldn't help but smile back.

"Welcome to the world's greatest service station. Cash or credit today?" the man at Charlie's window asked.

"Credit," said Charlie, handing a card out the window. "Fill it up, please," he added as he pulled the latch to open the hood.

"Sure thing, Mr. Charlie," the attendant replied brightly.

"But he knows you," protested the Area Manager, wondering if this was a special show put on for his benefit.

"Not really," replied Charlie. "He simply read my name on the credit card and then used it first chance he got. That's why his first question was 'Cash or credit?' Roughly ninety percent of their customers buy on credit, so they manage to call ninety percent of them by name. They soon learn the names of regular customers. Using names pays off for the attendants too. They get paid volume bonuses, and promotions to management jobs go to those who excel at frontline service."

The Area Manager was too impressed with what was happening outside the car to reply. But he wasn't surprised to learn that team members who looked after customers well were the ones to receive raises and promotions. He craned his neck from side to side, watching the two attendants at work. While one cleaned the windows and checked tire pressure, the other handled the hose and was at work under the hood.

The man whose name tag also carried the title PUMP ISLAND TEAM LEADER came to the window and reported. "Your oil is fine and so is the transmission fluid and coolant. The power steering took about two ounces. Be sure to get it checked the next time. All fan belts and hoses are fine. No charge for the power-steering fluid."

"Thanks," said Charlie.

As he left to top up the tank and turn off the pump, the other attendant, a woman, spoke to the Area Manager at his window.

"Are we going to win the big game tomorrow?" she asked as she polished the outside mirror.

"Of course we will," he declared without really knowing what game she was talking about and with enough enthusiasm to suit the need to support the hometown team.

"Hey. Right on," she replied. "You and I must be the only two who believe that they can do it. If Nelson's ready to play, we'll kill 'em," she continued as she handed a plastic bag through the window to the Area Manager, who was beginning to worry that his bravado in rooting for the hometown team had branded him a hopeless fool.

"Here's a fresh litter bag for your car," she said, mercifully switching from the game to the business at hand. "Do you have an old one I could get rid of for you?"

The Area Manager looked around. "I don't think so. Thanks anyway."

"No problem. That's what we're here for," said the woman, flashing him a warm smile. Again the Area Manager found himself smiling back.

"That's quite a smile you've got," he blurted out, and then felt immediately foolish. The woman, however, gave no sign of discomfort.

"Thanks," she said. "It's easy to smile when you're having a good time."

The Area Manager wondered how many people in service industries smiled at customers at all, much less because they were having a good time. At the service station where he bought gas, he was expected to pay for his gas before the pump was turned on, and then pump the gas into the car himself. As for smiles, he considered himself fortunate if the gum-chewing cashier bothered to acknowledge his presence with a grunt.

At the driver's window Charlie had just paid for the gas and was starting the car.

"Thanks for coming into the world's greatest service station, Mr. Charlie. I appreciate your business. Come back soon," the attendant said, looking Charlie straight in the eye and obviously meaning it.

"Will do," Charlie said. "Thanks for the great service."

"Anytime," came the reply. "That's what we're here for. And as you purchased more than ten gallons, we have a gift for you." He handed Charlie a half-price certificate for a nearby car wash and a second certificate for 10 percent off his next purchase.

"Thanks again," Charlie sang out as he drove off to the far side of the lot and parked so they could watch the pump island.

"Not bad for a service station, I'd say. What do you think?" Charlie asked.

"It's like what you see on TV when a race car pulls into a pit stop. And did you hear that woman? She said she was smiling because she was having a good time. And those uniforms were so bright and clean. But I noticed it was a brand-new station so I guess the uniforms were new too."

"The uniforms may be new but it's not a new station. Unless you call twelve years old new," said Charlie.

"Well, rebuilt or refurbished or whatever. It's the same thing."

"Aside from painting and maintenance it hasn't been touched in twelve years," said Charlie.

"Impossible," the Area Manager responded with conviction.

Charlie smiled but didn't argue further.

"Look at that self-serve on the corner," said the Area Manager, pointing across and down the street. "It is posting the same price as this full-serve. That's unusual."

"Actually, this full-serve is posting the same as the self-serve. The owner says his labor cost per gallon is as low or lower than the self-serve's and he always matches them in price," Charlie replied.

The Area Manager said, "Low prices, clean uniforms, free gifts—that whole system must be a big expense. I'm surprised they do it."

"Time to meet the man in charge. He can tell you if it pays. I suspect, though, that it may be the wrong question again."

Charlie swung around and parked at the side of the service station. A door marked OFFICE led to the second floor. Over the door was a sign that proclaimed: WELCOME TO THE HEAD OFFICE OF THE WORLD'S GREATEST SERVICE STATIONS.

Upstairs was tidy but cramped. Each employee had his or her own cubicle and all were wearing red shirts and gray slacks.

"Is Andrew in? I believe he's expecting us," said Charlie to the receptionist.

Looking up from her work, she smiled at Charlie and said in a very friendly soft manner, "Hello, sir. Nice to see you again. I'll let him know you're here."

The Area Manager was startled to see her turn in her chair, face the back of the office, and bellow with more lung power than he would have thought possible, "Andrew. They're here."

Turning back she said sweetly, and calmly. "Please have a seat. He'll be with you in a moment. Can I get you coffee?"

As they sat down Charlie whispered to the Area Manager, "When Andrew found out how much the telephone company was charging for the intercom feature on the phone system, he had it taken out."

People who create Raving Fans as customers have minds of their own, thought the Area Manager. No one can accuse them of being timid followers.

"You're right," said Charlie, again reading the Area Manager's thoughts. "But if they were follower types, they wouldn't be creating Raving Fans, would they?"

Their conversation was interrupted by another booming voice. "Charlie. Good to see you."

The Area Manager's head was tilted down to catch Charlie's whisper and he now began to lift his eyes to look at Andrew. By the time he was looking into Andrew's smiling face, his head was leaning back and he realized he was looking at one of the tallest men he had ever seen.

"Andrew played basketball," said Charlie.

"I'll bet," said the Area Manager.

"It's easier when you don't have to jump to reach the basket," Andrew said with a smile. "Go on in and sit down. I'll be with you in a minute."

Inside Andrew's office the Area Manager discovered, from the plaques and pictures on the wall, that Andrew had played with and for the best during his career. Mementos covered three of the four walls. The fourth was a large picture window, in front of which was Andrew's desk, positioned so he could see the pump island out front. The Area Manager wondered if constant vigilance by the boss accounted for the excellent service.

Andrew's arrival ended his perusal of the office and he again participated in the now familiar ritual of being introduced to an authentic customer service genius and discovering a fellow godchild of Charlie's.

"Nice to meet another brother," said Andrew, shaking the Area Manager's hand. He was honored to be called brother by a man who had played with the greats and was a customer service genius to boot.

"This time I agree. Andrew is a genius," Charlie said.

"You're too kind. Too kind. You're only saying that because it's true," responded Andrew with a chuckle.

Turning to the Area Manager, Andrew said, "I'm so perfect it's only my humble humility that makes me so likable."

"Customer service genius I grant," said Charlie. "As for perfect, you have much to be humble about."

The Area Manager couldn't help but admire the gentle good-natured banter between Charlie and the various people he had helped at some point in their careers. Andrew, he had learned, had been a pupil of Charlie's customer service campaign fifteen years earlier, and since then he had built his business from one service station to a chain of twenty.

"Enough about my perfection. At your age, Charlie, the wonder is that your eyes are good enough to even see me, let alone my perfection," Andrew said with a smile to Charlie.

Turning to the Area Manager he continued, "I bet you didn't come here to argue about my advanced state of perfection. I spotted Charlie's car gassing up a few minutes ago. Tell me, how was the service?"

"Mind-boggling," said the Area Manager. "I've never seen anything like it."

"Glad to hear it," said Andrew. "We do all of our training at this store. I know I can count on my other stores, but I always worry when Charlie brings someone here to show us off."

"I suspected your window was to spy on staff and that might be the third secret. But if your other stores are better than this one, that's obviously not the reason," the Area Manager admitted.

"It's my spy window all right," said Andrew with a laugh. "I use it to spy on customers. Every day I go to a different store and pump gas for at least an hour to listen to customers. The rest of the day I have the window to remind me why I'm doing all the telephoning and paperwork."

"Well, if you're not spying on staff to keep them running, tell me how you do it," he quizzed Andrew.

"With the third secret of creating Raving Fans, of course. I take it you're interested in learning it," teased Andrew.

"Right on," said the Area Manager eagerly, and as he had when he learned the first two secrets, he found himself edging forward on his chair with anticipation.

"No doubt you've noticed that the market secret builds on the first, the source secret. The third, the experience secret, builds on the first two. Are you ready?" questioned Andrew.

"You bet," replied the Area Manager.

"Okay. Here it is. Simple and powerful. The third secret is **Deliver Plus One**.

The Area Manager found this third secret as puzzling as the first two had been initially. And he was a bit disappointed he hadn't been told to look at his bracelet. He had checked to make sure that only the first two secrets were on the shield when he put it on that morning.

"This third secret may be short and to the point. But I confess I don't know what the point is," he said.

"My fault really," said Charlie. "But Leo says a bigger shield would look all wrong, so of course he wins and I wind up with a three-word secret. But it fits," Charlie concluded with an apologetic shrug.

The Area Manager was trying to make some sense out of what Charlie had just said when Andrew intervened. "Take a look at your shield."

The Area Manager quickly looked at the shield. There it was. Right below the second secret:

The three words just fit the space. At the same time he was astonished by the sudden appearance of the writing.

"Let me explain," continued Andrew. "Before Leo started handing out the bracelets, the third secret was, and really still is, **Deliver the Vision Plus One Percent.** But as you can see, it won't fit and still be readable, so it's been shortened to **Deliver Plus One.**"

"Sounds like a clear case of Leo's vision of a bracelet bumping very close to the 'take a hike' edge of Charlie's customer service window," suggested the Area Manager with a smile.

"The razor's edge," agreed Charlie.

"Well, if it makes you feel any better, I've got to tell you that the full secret isn't a whole lot clearer to me than the short one."

"Let's look at it," said Andrew. "The secret says two things. First, it tells you to deliver. Not sometimes, not most times. But all the time. No exceptions contemplated or allowed. Second, it talks about 'plus one percent.' I'll come back to that, but first of all we have to talk about delivery."

"Consistency, consistency, consistency," interjected Charlie. "Consistency is critical. Consistency creates credibility. My pro will explain how it works. Andrew, if you please."

"With pleasure, Charlie," said Andrew. "As Charlie told you, consistency is key to delivering Raving Fan Service. When you're creating Raving Fans it's a fragile relationship. They've been burned before and they don't trust easily. You're trying to pull them in and they're usually trying to resist. Consistency will overcome resistance, but in the meantime they're watching like a hawk for you to mess up."

"Really? Can you give me an example?" asked the Area Manager.

"Every new service we introduce is an example," replied Andrew. "Take washing windows. My vision is to have the glass polished inside and out with all the necessary chemicals at hand to remove road tar and bugs and even the wax residue left by car washes. The first vision we had from customers was that they'd like to have a bucket of clean water and a squeegee so they could wipe off their own window. For many it was just water—any kind of water! Clean water was too much to hope for.

"When we started, team members cleaned only the windshield. I forbade them to touch any other window unless specifically asked by a customer. And customers were aware of getting their windshield cleaned and how good a job we were doing. Some would almost glare until the window was well cleaned. It was as if they were waiting for us to fail so they could pounce on us."

"And do they pounce?" the Area Manager asked with a smile. He was thinking of a customer crouched like a cat, ready to spring at Andrew. Given Andrew's size, he decided it would have to be a very brave or foolish customer.

"They let us know when we missed," Andrew assured him. "Sometimes angrily, sometimes politely, and one customer just drove off without paying! He telephoned later and told us that when we advertised a clean windshield, he felt the price we charged was for both gas and a clean windshield. And he was right. He said if we didn't wash his windshield, he didn't feel he should be expected to pay. He felt he'd been cheated.

"I'm sure we lost customers who never said anything at all. Think about it. We started a new service that was virtually unavailable anywhere else and was a free bonus. Yet when we failed to deliver perfection, customers got angry or left us. And they didn't have any better place to go—or even as good a place."

"All because you weren't consistent," said Charlie. "Customers count all right. They count on you to do what you say you'll do."

"Charlie's right," said Andrew. "You have to walk your talk, as they say. It would have been a disaster to try to clean all the windows at first. We failed to deliver too often as it was. If we had tried to wash all the windows, our failure rate would have been much higher, and it would have taken us much longer to improve. But little by little we became consistently good. Then we started to wash all the windows. Now our customers can rely on us. Clean windows every time without fail wins us Raving Fans."

"Sounds like what you are saying is 'Don't offer too much service, at least at the start,' " said the Area Manager.

"Exactly," replied Andrew. "To start with, limit the number of areas where you want to make a difference. First, it allows you to be consistent. Second, you'll be much further ahead doing a bang-up job on one thing rather than introducing a whole string of customer service goals all at once. You'll never bring it off. It just can't be done that way."

"As always, Andrew's on the money," said Charlie. "You can always build toward the total vision once you're successful with one or two things, but it's difficult, if not impossible, to try to change too much at once."

"Airlines are always making that mistake," said the Area Manager. "They keep advertising new things but they can't even get the old ones right. For example, they promise me a choice for dinner. I bet they started that five years ago. But then when I fly, I find they don't have enough of each meal to make sure I really do get a choice. That annoys me. I'd be much happier if they'd just give me any decent meal and then bring me my coffee within fifteen minutes of the food tray arriving."

Charlie again broke in. "That airline story shows there are two kinds of small. There's few in number and there's small in size. You may be trying to do one thing, like offer a choice of meals, but it may be too big or difficult to get right all at once. There is no sense in doing just one thing if the size of the service promise is too large to successfully implement quickly. Better to find a smaller thing, a smaller service promise, you can deliver consistently."

Andrew, who had been waiting for Charlie to finish, said, "If an airline says they're going to give me a choice for dinner and they don't, it makes me mad. Better they should keep their mouths shut, and not set themselves up for failure. They spend a fortune on advertising a service they don't provide, so you feel ripped off when you don't get it. Not a very bright way to spend money to improve customer service."

"What you're saying is 'Promise less than you deliver.' I learned that in a marketing course I took last year," said the Area Manager.

"Not really," replied Andrew. "Some say that's good advice. Perhaps it is if what you want is a satisfied customer. But I don't want satisfied customers and I don't like that advice. As far as I'm concerned, that's like saying the way to create better basketball players is to install bigger basket hoops."

"But aren't you cutting back when you clean only the windshield before doing the other windows?" challenged the Area Manager.

"Not at all," said Andrew. "I wasn't promising less when I set out to clean every windshield. I was promising more than I was then doing. What I didn't do was put the hurdle too high to start with and I didn't raise the hurdle until we could consistently deliver. What you have to do is promise more and deliver more. Just don't promise too much at once."

"In some ways, though, that is promising less," persisted the Area Manager.

"It is," agreed Andrew. "It's promising less than the impossible. If that's what you understand by 'promise less,' fine, but it's too negative for my liking. To create Raving Fans, don't drive promises down. Drive delivery up.

"Regardless of what you promise, though, it's consistency that's important. Customers allow themselves to be seduced into becoming Raving Fans only when they know they can count on you time and time again."

"That's interesting," said the Area Manager. "If I understand you correctly, you're saying that exceeding expectations is important but it's even more important to consistently meet expectations."

"Meet first. Exceed second," said Andrew. "It should be tattooed on the inside eyelids of every manager in the country," he joked.

"The worst thing you can do is meet expectations one time, fall short another, and exceed every now and then. I guarantee you'll drive your customers nuts and into the hands of the competition first chance they get."

"So how do I ensure consistency?" asked the Area Manager.

"To be consistent you have to have systems," replied Andrew. "At the core of every great customer service organization is a package of systems and a training program to inculcate those systems into the soul of that company. That's what guarantees consistency.

"Delivering your product or service properly time after time after time without fail is the foundation of Raving Fan customer service. Systems are what allows you to guarantee delivery—not smiles and 'Have a nice day.' "

"Sounds like you're a Raving Fan of systems and training," laughed the Area Manager.

"I sure am," agreed Andrew with a smile. "I learned the importance of systems when I played basketball. 'Plays' in basketball or football are really systems. I also learned that all the systems in the world aren't worth a pinch of salt if everyone isn't trained to follow them."

"You run your company this way?" asked the Area Manager.

"We do," said Andrew. "For example, when we tell our team members to be friendly to customers, we help by training them in exactly what they can do to project a friendly image."

"You mean there are specific things you train them to do that make them friendly?" asked the Area Manager.

"Of course. For example, our research shows friendly people talk about topics not directly connected with the business transaction at hand and so we train team members to do just that," said Andrew.

"The attendant who gave me the litter bag asked which team would win the 'big game' tomorrow," said the Area Manager, realizing how that simple exchange really had seemed friendly, even when he didn't know anything about the game.

"Good for her. Talking about things not related to the gasoline purchase is part of our customer service package," said Andrew with evident pleasure.

"But that's just one example of how we have systems to keep us consistent. We have a training room where new team members spend ten hours learning how we do things before they go near a customer. When we take your credit card or check your oil, you can count on our doing it by our system. No surprises. No disappointments."

The Area Manager considered for a moment what Andrew had said and then asked, "I can see why systems are important. But don't you run the risk of turning your team members into robots? Wouldn't they become wooden?"

"Wooden robots like basketball players? Basketball players have systems, but they have to be able to go beyond the system, change the play, when it can help the team and score points. It's the same for our team members. The systems set the guidelines. However, our team members know that delivering Raving Fan Service means sometimes they have to alter the play to better serve the customer and they're encouraged to do just that."

"How would that work?" asked the Area Manager.

"Let's take talking about nonbusiness-related matters again," said Andrew. "While doing that is part of our system, what they talk about, and when, is up to them. Or they can decide to step right out of the system. Sometimes customers are in a big hurry and would feel any extra talk was delaying them. Our team members have to judge that.

"What we have are systems. Not rules. Rules create robots. Not systems. Systems are predetermined ways to achieve a result. The emphasis has to be on achieving the result, not the system for the system's sake. That's the difference between systems and rules. With a rule the emphasis is on the procedure, not necessarily the result. We have rules about smoking within ten feet of a gasoline pump. We have systems for delivering service.

"The purpose of systems is to ensure consistency, not create robots. Rules do that. Our team members have to create the Raving Fan experience for our customers every time. Systems give you a floor, not a ceiling," concluded Andrew.

Charlie, who had been nodding his agreement as Andrew talked, spoke up. "Systems allow you to deliver a minimum standard of performance consistently. That's important because if you fall short of what you've said you'll do, you've cheated the customer."

"Strong language," observed the Area Manager.

"Strong feelings," Charlie shot back.

"Once you're consistent, ongoing improvement is equally important," said Andrew.

"That's where the Plus One Percent comes in, I'll bet," said the Area Manager. "That one percent puzzles me. It hardly seems worth it."

"The one percent is to keep you moving ahead and focused beyond your vision," said Andrew.

"Is that why you greet customers by name? To go beyond your vision?" asked the Area Manager.

"No way," replied Andrew. "I'm just getting started. The vision is to have a whole bunch of people waving flags and cheering each customer by name as they drive in."

"You'll never do it. That's crazy. Surely there must be some test of reasonableness to the vision," said the Area Manager.

"Of course there is. If it serves a customer need it's valid. There's no such thing as too good, as long as it's within what you choose to define as your window of customer service. And there's no such thing as never. There's always a way to do it."

"But a crowd of people waving flags? That's impossible."

Charlie spoke up, "Seems to me that's what you said earlier about what Andrew's already doing."

"That's right," agreed the Area Manager cautiously. "But I've got to tell you, the thought of being greeted by a flag-waving crowd would be enough to make me go elsewhere. I don't see why you would do it."

"Do it?" exclaimed Andrew. "Who says I'm doing it? I'm telling you what my vision is. Before I actually do anything, I have to discover what the customer really wants. If my customers feel as you do, I'll alter my vision. It wouldn't be the first time I've altered after finding out what the customer really wants."

"I doubt it matters," suggested the Area Manager. "Even if you wanted to do it, I'd still say it was impossible."

"I know it sounds impossible, but believe me, so was greeting customers with running team members and calling each customer by name at first. I didn't have any idea how I was going to do those things either. They initially seemed impossible, but I did them by using The Rule of One Percent from the third secret."

"The Rule of One Percent?"

"Earlier you said one percent didn't seem worth it. Well, from where I sit, one percent is the magic number. The biggest problem I have in delivering my vision is knowing what to do next. Either I try to do too much at once and get frustrated or I sit immobilized because of the size of the job ahead. The rule of one percent reminds me that all I have to do is to improve by one percent. That I can do. If I improve one percent next week and again the week after that, by the end of the year I'm ahead by more than fifty percent."

The Area Manager's face reflected his pleasure at this discovery. "The Rule of One Percent could really make things happen," he said. "I'll start using it the minute I'm back in the office."

"You don't have to wait for the office," said Andrew. "You can make big changes in almost anything or achieve great things in your life by improving or changing one percent. Things can't help but improve if you keep at it one percent at a time."

Charlie had been nodding with approval and now added, "One percent has a second big advantage. Ongoing one-percent improvement will take you a long way from where you started, but it also means you don't blindly set a course and then follow it. One percent allows you to add the magic ingredient that guarantees improvement rather than just change."

Charlie fell silent and sat gazing out the window. "Come on, Charlie," said the Area Manager impatiently, "I'm not a mind reader like you. What's the magic ingredient?"

"Flexibility," said Charlie with such reverence you could be forgiven for assuming he was talking about golf. "More customer service hopes have been wrecked on the rigid shores of immobile bureaucratic minds than anywhere else."

Andrew smiled and commented, "A touch poetic, but I suppose it's a fault one has to expect from a Fairy Godmother. The point Charlie makes is important, though. We've already talked about how the team members have to be flexible and change systems when necessary. The vision also has to be changing. Always developing. Visions do only two things. They grow or they die. And when visions die, it's customer service that gets buried. You have to be ready to change direction when the vision changes, and one percent allows you to alter course. You're not locked in, head down, driving one way, blindly pursuing a big goal, only to find when you arrive that the customer moved the goal posts some time ago."

"Dead visions! Buried service! Head-down driving! And I'm accused of being too poetic," sniffed Charlie before continuing seriously. "The reason the three secrets emphasize a changing vision is that only an up-to-the-minute vision can hope to create Raving Fans. The perfect vision isn't a frozen picture of the future. Customers' needs and wants change all the time."

The Area Manager nodded his head. "That's easy for me to understand. My uncle made garden hoses. You'd think garden hose would be pretty standard stuff, but I remember his telling me his customers always wanted something different. He was always changing his extrusion dies and even the raw material that went into the hoses."

The same was true for any organization or business, Andrew told the Area Manager. "My dad ran a motion-picture theater. He said his customers could go from Texas to New York faster than an express train. On Friday night the customers' vision might be a Western, and Saturday those same customers would have a Broadway musical vision of perfection."

When Charlie first identified flexibility as the magic ingredient, the Area Manager thought this would conflict with the gospel of consistency Charlie and Bill had been preaching earlier. Now he understood that flexibility had to do with *what* was delivered as part of the customer service product. Consistency had to do with *how* it was delivered.

The importance of change was so evident to the Area Manager that he was puzzled at why others didn't see things as clearly. "It seems obvious to me that yesterday's vision isn't going to be valid today. Yet you say rigid bureaucratic minds wreck customer service. How can that be? Why would anyone stick with an out-of-date vision?"

"Laziness, stupidity, stuck in a rut, closed-minded, love of tradition, fear of the future, bullheaded, pigheaded, noheaded, who knows?" said Charlie with a shrug of his shoulders. "Two things are for sure, however. One, those people aren't listening to customers, and two, they don't want Raving Fans."

Andrew spoke up. "A Raving Fan relationship goes far beyond your company's product. If you don't listen to your customer's thoughts to learn his needs and desires, you fail to give him what he needs as a product because you simply don't know what that need really is. Further, you reject him as a person. By not listening to him, you're saying his thoughts have no value.

"Look what happens when you turn it around. First, you can serve your customers' needs because now you know what they really are. Second, you've asked, listened to, and respected their opinions. You're treating them like intelligent human beings. That's powerful."

"Very powerful," agreed Charlie. "The Rule of One Percent tells you how to move ahead and then go beyond the vision. It also lets you constantly monitor the customers' needs and alter your direction when they alter theirs. Listening to customers is powerful, just as Andrew says. Responding to what customers say is dynamite."

The Area Manager was sitting so that he could see the pump island through Andrew's window. Cars were arriving and team members were running. "It's really a human relationship, isn't it?" he said. "It's not really customers and company. It's not even customers and employees. It's just people and people. People arrive with needs and people go out and serve them to fulfill those needs."

Charlie and Andrew looked at each other with happy smiles on their faces.

After a short silence the Area Manager continued, "Customers have needs beyond the need of the company's product, whether it comes in a box or is a particular service. People need to feel they belong to the group. People need to feel that they're important and that what they do, think, and say truly matters.

"Andrew calls them by name; Leo pins a flower on them and assumes they're honest when they try on clothes in his store. Bill hunts out and listens to every customer from the loading dock to the president, and Sally shines their shoes and shows them how to save money and eat a healthy diet. Dennis opens the car door. What they're all doing is giving their customers a symbolic hug."

"Deliver that kind of hug with everything else you've learned and you'll create Raving Fans for sure," said Andrew. "It's all about people. I've never heard it put better."

"Time for a graduation ceremony," said Charlie with pride. "We've got ourselves a graduate with honors this time, if I do say so myself."

While the two teachers congratulated themselves on their fine accomplishment, their prize student was scarcely aware of their presence. He continued to stare out the window and think about all he had learned.

The three secrets all fit together. He understood the importance of having a vision of his own to start with. He saw the necessity of then talking to customers. For the first time he felt he knew what talking to customers really meant and how to listen, even to silences. He also knew when to implement what customers wanted, and when to ignore customers' wants.

Best of all, he knew how to take this vision and turn it into an action plan. Consistency alongside ongoing improvement plus the ability to alter course quickly were keys to creating Raving Fans. Promise more only up to the point you can deliver consistently and then deliver more using The Rule of One Percent. That was the way to go. That was the way to do it.

Before meeting Charlie he had viewed his company's product in a very narrow way and saw customer service as some sort of extra. Part of the packaging—to be thrown away when opened. Now he understood that his company's product was a lot more than one dimensional. It was not just a piece of merchandise. It also included service. Good or bad, like it or not, his company had a customer service product that was both how well the merchandise suited the customers' needs and the human dimension of the customer/company relationship.

Having considered this, the Area Manager turned back to Charlie and Andrew with new confidence. "What's this about a graduation ceremony?" he asked.

"Age-old tradition," replied a solemn Charlie. "At one time it was held in the Great Hall of Hosts. Choirs sang, I delivered the address, and certificates were awarded. We do better now."

"Better?" questioned the Area Manager, thrilled at the thought of what might await him.

"Yes, much better," said Charlie, breaking into a broad grin. "We play golf."

Andrew and Charlie set the graduation game for the next week when Andrew told them he would be in their area. "I'll call Sally and Bill," promised Charlie. "You'd best drop in to say hello to Leo yourself," he said to the Area Manager. "He never plays golf."

As with the first two secrets, once the lesson was ended, Charlie was anxious to leave and the Area Manager found himself saying good-bye.

"I know I'm a long way away," said Andrew to the Area Manager as he walked them to the door, "but if you're ever in the area, come visit. In the meantime, you've got my phone number. I expect to hear from you regularly and I'll be calling you."

"I'll do that," said the Area Manager.

The trip home was no less spectacular than the arrival. This time the Area Manager kept his eyes open while they went through. One minute he was driving away from Andrew's, the next he was hurtling down his home interstate.

The passage, said Charlie, was quite simple. Apparently it had something to do with space bending back on itself. All you had to do, said Charlie, was find the point at which where you were bent and touched where you wanted to be, and cross over. "When two spatial planes bump into each other, a hole or two always opens up. You have to keep your wits about you, though. I lost two centuries one afternoon when I wasn't paying attention and found the folk back then decidedly unhappy with my sudden arrival," explained Charlie in a matter-of-fact manner.

"I'm glad you waited until we were safely back to tell me about the navigation hazards," said the Area Manager as Charlie dropped him at his office.

The Area Manager was delighted to be back and put all three secrets to work instead of just the first two. When his people were gathered together he announced, "We've got a lot of work ahead of us, ladies and gentleman. We're going to improve one percent around here. Let me explain."

And explain he did. By the time the graduation golf ceremony took place, he was well under way with his Raving Fan Action Plan. Following the advice to start small, and The Rule of One Percent, he had the full support of everyone who worked for him. Although what the Area Manager was proposing would eventually be a massive shift, no one felt threatened by the small start and a goal of one percent improvement.

The employees also embraced creating Raving Fans as part of the company's culture, not just another program—here today and gone tomorrow—to be replaced by the next program-of-the-month mandated by the Head Office.

The day of the graduation game was perfect. Warm, with a light breeze. The Area Manager played so well he was sure Charlie must have been rewarding him with a little help.

As they walked off the 18th green, Charlie reached into the side pocket of his golf bag and pulled out a small presentation case.

"Will you kindly do the honors?" he asked Sally, holding out the case to her.

"With pleasure," she replied and opened the case. She removed a silver lapel pin, which the Area Manager instantly recognized. Each of the people Charlie had taken him to visit had been wearing one, but until this moment he hadn't made the connection.

"Congratulations," said Sally as she attached the pin to the lapel of the Area Manager's shirt. "You are now officially designated a 'Charlie,' the highest customer service honor there is. You may place the designation 'Chas.' behind your name, hand out Charlie Awards to deserving persons or organizations, and teach the three secrets of creating Raving Fans to all wishing to learn."

With that, Charlie lifted his putter, and resting it gently first on the Area Manager's left and then right shoulder, he solemnly intoned, "I hereby proclaim you 'Charlie' with all the rights and privileges thereto appertaining."

"I'm honored," the Area Manager replied. "Tell me, what are these rights and privileges?"

"Ah," said Charlie with a mischievous grin. "You have the right to summon me to golf at any time and you now have the privilege of buying us all a drink."

"As I said, I'm honored," laughed the Area Manager.

Back at the clubhouse, the Area Manager sat on the veranda with Charlie and his newfound friends. Bill, the plant manager, was unable to golf with the Area Manager, Charlie, Sally, and Andrew, but he joined them for a drink. When Leo also showed up for a drink, everyone assured the Area Manager that this was a great honor indeed. The Area Manager told them of his progress creating Raving Fans and felt good about their congratulations and advice.

Eventually he fell silent. The others, sensing something, let the conversation die.

"I don't know how to thank you for all you've done," the Area Manager said with evident appreciation. "I know you're my friends now. I feel like a member of a family. You've helped me with your gifts of knowledge and friendship and you've asked for nothing—expected nothing—in return."

After a few moments he looked at Charlie and said quietly, "Charlie, you've been both friend and mentor. I trust you'll keep in touch."

Charlie, whose Fairy Godmothering skills had never extended to coping with the honest heartfelt emotion side of the business—simply because he was too sentimental—blustered with a reply in the best Charlie fashion: "In touch. Of course I'll be in touch. You still golf, don't you? My Heavens, yes. I'll be in touch. The follow-up alone will be for ages and then there are regular monitoring sessions. Yes, yes, I'll be in touch. I see great things in your future, my friend. Great things indeed."

The Area Manager replied, "I'll see if I can't deliver that vision plus one percent, Charlie."

"I'm sure you will. I'm sure you will," answered Charlie.

And the Area Manager did deliver. Soon his area topped the company's charts and the Head Office began receiving letters from customers who were so pleased that they felt they just had to write a thank-you note to the President.

One day the President called the Area Manager into her office. "I've learned our Executive Vice-President has decided to retire at the end of the year," she said. "The Board has asked me to recommend a successor able to follow me when I retire in three years, and as I own eighty percent of the voting stock, I think they'll give some weight to my recommendation. I've given them your name. You're a customer service genius and I want you to do for the company what you've done for your department. Tell me, where will you start?"

"Well," said the Area Manager beaming with pleasure, "let's just close our eyes and spend a few minutes visualizing our customers using our products."

Charlie Awards

Ken and Sheldon are Raving Fans of . . .

Richard L. M. "Dick" Dawson and **Kerry L. Hawkins,** of Cargill Limited, for their support and suggestions and for providing a forum to test many of the creating Raving Fans ideas with Cargill's Canadian management team—Charlies all.

Hugh Goldie, of the Robert Thompson Partnership, who was first to read the manuscript and offered excellent advice.

Chris Hemmeter, of Hemmeter Partners, who taught us to listen to the music as well as the lyrics.

Richard Kroft, of Tryton Investment Company Limited, whose Controlled Environments Ltd. has provided many examples of Raving Fan Service.

Ted Ransby, of Great-West Life Assurance Company, who has contributed excellent advice and given freely of his experience.

As well as the many additional people who have read this book as it was being written, offering comments, criticisms, and suggestions—in particular, Trevor Cochrane, Carl Eisbrenner, Derek Johannson, Ray Kives, Bob May, Michael Nozick, Maureen Prendiville, Hartley Richardson, Ross Robinson, and Jim Tennant.

Ken and Sheldon also acknowledge the contribution of:

Larry Hughes, of Morrow, whose patience, nurturing, and skill with the English language are legendary in the publishing industry and much appreciated by the authors.

Bob Nelson, vice president of Blanchard Training and Development, Inc., whose fine editorial hand, tenacity, and drive to make things happen have made this book a reality.

Margret McBride, of Margret McBride Literary Agency, friend, associate, collaborator, adviser, coach, and confidante.

Rita Loewen, secretary to Sheldon Bowles, who has patiently typed and pushed the book ahead.

Eleanor Terndrup, Dana Kyle, Dee Kelly, and **Dorothy Morris,** the support staff to Ken and Margie, who are always ready to help and have Raving Fans inside and outside of Blanchard Training and Development.

Frances Bowles, who has read, edited, and cheered as this book progressed. Her support has been unfailing.

Ian and Sandy McLandress, who have for years met Sheldon and Penny at six A.M. for a four-mile brisk walk before breakfast. They have trudged through snow, sleet, rain, and heat, listening to ideas and offering encouragement as this book went back and forth between San Diego and Winnipeg.

About the Authors

Ken Blanchard has had a tremendous impact on the day-to-day management of people and companies.

As a writer in the field of management, his impact has been far reaching. His One Minute Manager Library, which includes *The One Minute Manager®* (1982), *Putting the One Minute Manager® to Work* (1984), *Leadership and the One Minute Manager®* (1985), *The One Minute Manager® Gets Fit* (1986), *The One Minute Manager® Meets the Monkey* (1989), and *The One Minute Manager® Builds High-Performing Teams* (1990), has collectively sold more than seven million copies and has been translated into more than twenty languages. He is also co-author with Dr. Paul Hersey of *Management of Organizational Behavior,* a classic textbook now in its fifth edition, and with Dr. Norman Vincent Peale of *The Power of Ethical Management* (1988).

Blanchard is chairman of Blanchard Training and Development, Inc., a full-service management consulting and training company, which he founded in 1979 with his wife, Marjorie. He also maintains a faculty position in leadership at the University of Massachusetts, Amherst, and a visiting lectureship at Cornell University, where he is also an elected member of the Board of Trustees.

Sheldon Bowles began his career as a newspaper reporter. He has covered stories in the Canadian Arctic, Japan, the United States, and Europe for such diverse media as *The Toronto Globe and Mail,* the Canadian Broadcasting Corporation, *Time, The Times* (London), and *The Winnipeg Free Press.* He left reporting to gain business experience and joined Royal Canadian Securities Limited, where he rose to become a director and vice-president. For fifteen years he was the president and CEO of Domo Gasoline Corporation Ltd., which he built—along with Senator Douglas Everett, chairman—into one of Canada's largest independent gasoline retailers with many hundreds of employees. At a time when the industry was going almost exclusively self-serve, they built their business and reputation on full-serve "Jump to the Pump"® service.

Sheldon sold his business interests several years ago so that he might enjoy a third career before reaching fifty. He now spends his time writing, speaking to various groups and organizations, and serving on the boards of several companies and community organizations. He is a true Raving Fan of Penny, his wife of twenty-six years, and along with their two children, Kingsley and Patti, they divide their time between their home in Winnipeg and summer homes in Kenora and Willard Lake, Ontario.

Services Available

Ken Blanchard and Sheldon Bowles speak to conventions and organizations all over the world. They also have their messages available on audio and video tape.

In addition, Blanchard Training and Development, Inc., conducts seminars and in-depth consulting in the areas of customer service, leadership, performance management, and quality.

For further information on Dr. Blanchard's and Sheldon Bowles's activities and programs contact:

Blanchard Training and Development, Inc.
125 State Place
Escondido, CA 92025
(800) 728-6000 or (619) 489-5005
(619) 489-8407 (fax)

Sheldon Bowles
Ode to Joy Limited
5-165 Kennedy Street
Winnipeg R3C 156
Manitoba, Canada
(204) 947-0406
(204) 947-1536 (fax)

ᴜᴹ WILLIAM MORROW
An Imprint of HarperCollins*Publishers* • www.harpercollins.com

THE BLANCHARD & BOWLES BUSINESS LIBRARY
PERFORMANCE DEVELOPMENT

RAVING FANS
A Revolutionary Approach to Customer Service
ISBN 0-688-12316-3 (hardcover)

An invaluable handbook for delivering stunning customer service and achieving bottom line results.

GUNG HO!
Turn On the People in Any Organization
ISBN 0-688-15428-X (hardcover)

Learn how to energize and motivate employees to create a "gung ho" organization.

BIG BUCKS!
How to Make Serious Money for Both You and Your Company
ISBN 0-688-17035-8 (hardcover)
ISBN 0-694-52365-8 (abridged audio CD)
ISBN 0-694-52366-6 (unabridged cassette)

A simple yet powerful guide for creating lasting wealth.

HIGH FIVE!
The Magic of Working Together
ISBN 0-688-17036-6 (hardcover)
ISBN 0-694-52486-7 (unabridged audio CD)
ISBN 0-694-52485-9 (unabridged cassette)

Brilliantly illustrates the dynamics of teamwork.

Available wherever books are sold, or call 1-800-331-3761 to order.

THE BLANCHARD & BOWLES BUSINESS LIBRARY

THE CLASSIC

Increase Productivity, Profits, and Your Own Prosperity

The **One Minute Manager**

Kenneth Blanchard, Ph.D.
Spencer Johnson, M.D.

A Classic!
Whether you manage a home, a business, a family, or a life . . . it works!

THE ONE MINUTE MANAGER®

ISBN 0-688-01429-1 (hardcover)
Learn the management techniques that have helped
thousands of top managers and Fortune 500 companies
build productivity and profitability.

Available wherever books are sold, or call 1-800-331-3761 to order.